# Dave Matthews Band
## ANTHOLOGY
### CONTENTS

| | SONG | ALBUM |
|---|---|---|
| 2 | American Baby | *Stand Up* |
| 8 | Ants Marching | *Under the Table and Dreaming* |
| 16 | The Best of What's Around | *Under the Table and Dreaming* |
| 22 | Crash into Me | *Crash* |
| 33 | Crush | *Before These Crowded Streets* |
| 42 | Dancing Nancies | *Under the Table and Dreaming* |
| 53 | Digging a Ditch | *Busted Stuff* |
| 61 | Don't Drink the Water | *Before These Crowded Streets* |
| 69 | The Dreaming Tree | *Before These Crowded Streets* |
| 79 | Everybody Wake Up (Our Finest Hour Arrives) | *Stand Up* |
| 86 | Everyday | *Everyday* |
| 91 | Grace Is Gone | *Busted Stuff* |
| 99 | Grey Street | *Busted Stuff* |
| 106 | Hunger For the Great Light | *Stand Up* |
| 113 | I Did It | *Everyday* |
| 119 | Jimi Thing | *Under the Table and Dreaming* |
| 126 | Louisiana Bayou | *Stand Up* |
| 133 | Out of My Hands | *Stand Up* |
| 139 | Rapunzel | *Before These Crowded Streets* |
| 147 | Satellite | *Under the Table and Dreaming* |
| 152 | Say Goodbye | *Crash* |
| 161 | So Much to Say | *Crash* |
| 168 | So Right | *Everyday* |
| 176 | The Space Between | *Everyday* |
| 184 | Stay (Wasting Time) | *Before These Crowded Streets* |
| 193 | Steady As We Go | *Stand Up* |
| 197 | Too Much | *Crash* |
| 206 | Tripping Billies | *Crash* |
| 212 | Two Step | *Crash* |
| 219 | Warehouse | *Under the Table and Dreaming* |
| 230 | What Would You Say | *Under the Table and Dreaming* |
| 235 | Where Are You Going | *Busted Stuff* |

Approved by the Dave Matthews Band

Photography by Danny Clinch

Piano/Vocal arrangements by John Nicholas

Cherry Lane Music Company
Director of Publications/Project Editor: Mark Phillips
Manager of Publications: Gabrielle Fastman

ISBN-13: 978-1-57560-972-0
ISBN-10: 1-57560-972-X

*Visit our website at www.cherrylane.com*

# American Baby

Words and Music by
Dave Matthews Band and Mark Batson

**Moderately fast**

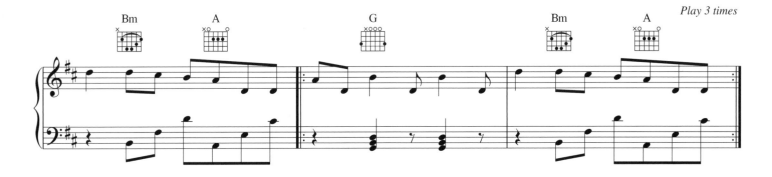

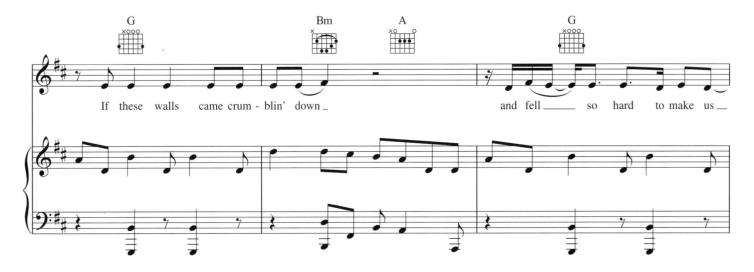

If these walls came crum-blin' down ___ and fell ___ so hard to make us ___

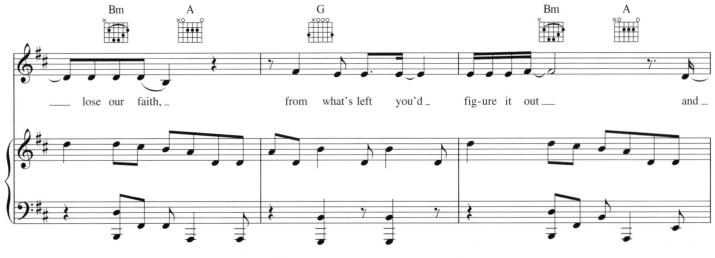

___ lose our faith, ___ from what's left you'd ___ fig-ure it out ___ and ___

still make lem-on-ade taste like a sun-ny day. ___ Stay, _____

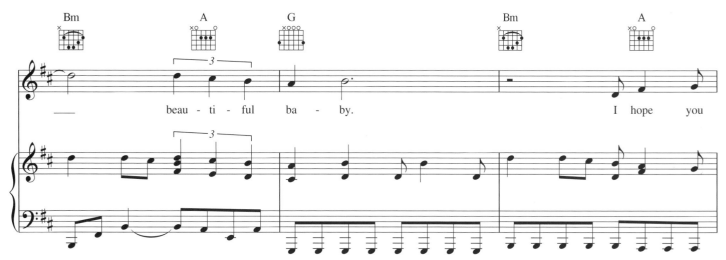

___ beau - ti - ful ba - by. ___ I hope you

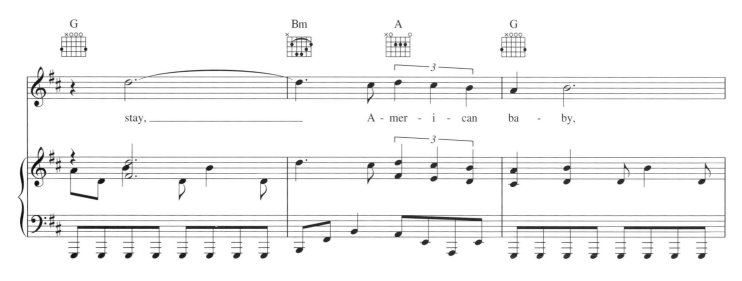

stay, _____ A - mer - i - can ba - by,

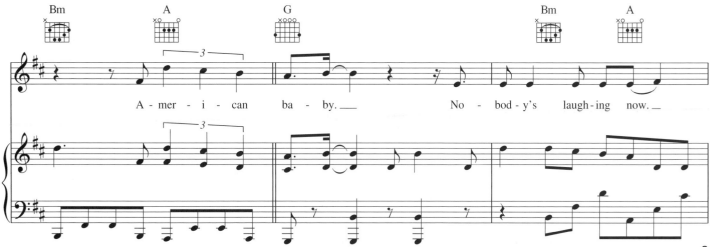

A - mer - i - can ba - by. ___ No - bod - y's laugh-ing now. ___

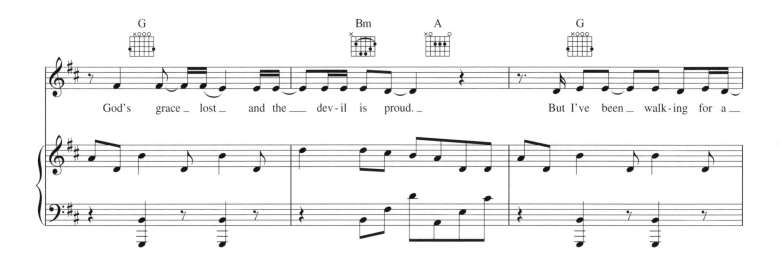

God's grace _ lost _ and the _ dev-il is proud. _ But I've been _ walk-ing for a _

_ thou-sand miles. One last time I could _ see you smile. _

I, I _ hold, hold _ on to you. _ You bring _ me hope. _

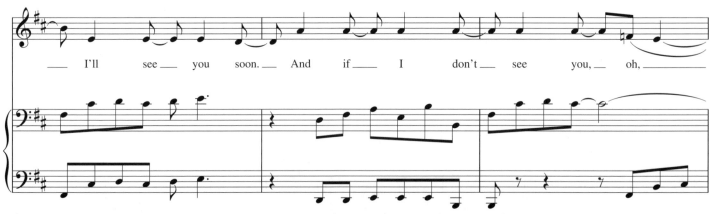

_ I'll see _ you soon. And if _ I don't _ see you, _ oh, _

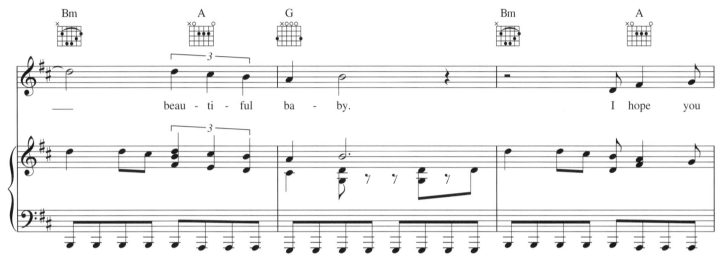

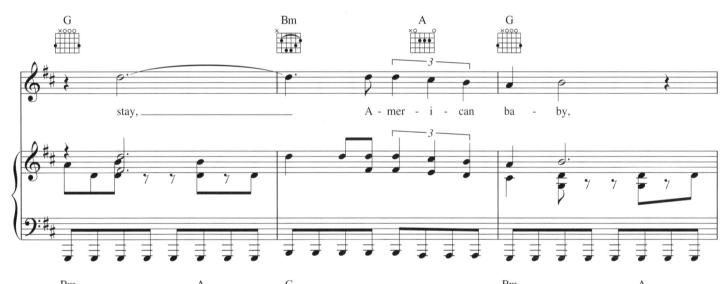

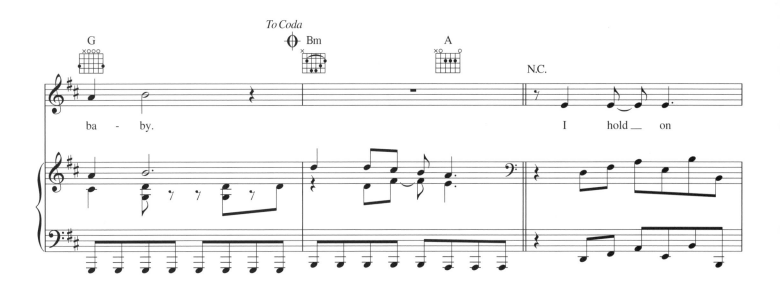

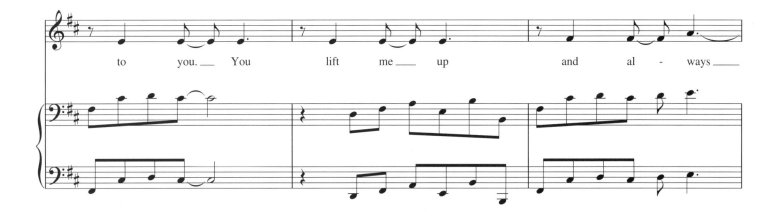

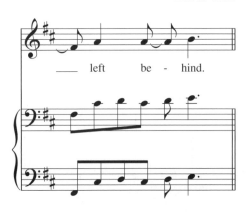

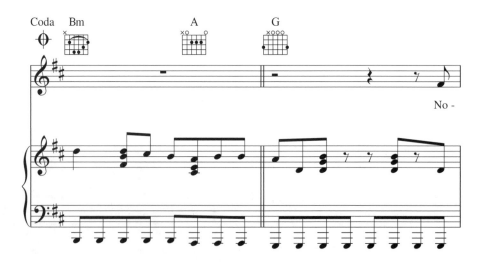

bod - y's laugh - ing now,    but you could al - ways make me laugh out ___ loud.

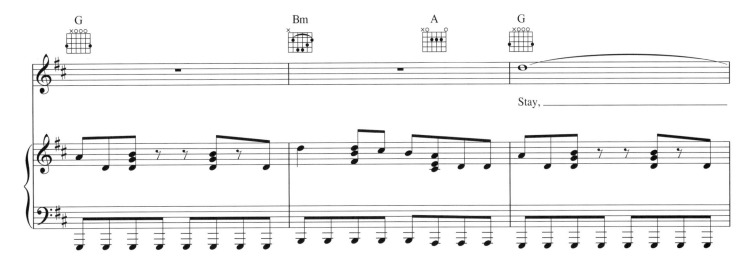

Stay, _____

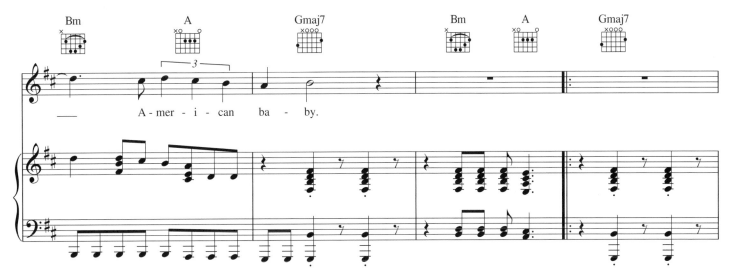

___ A - mer - i - can ba - by.

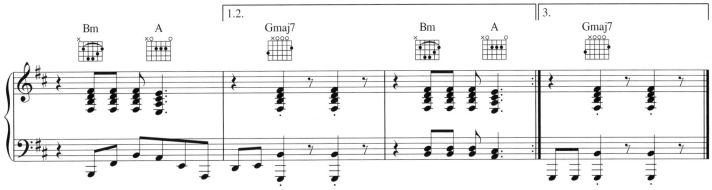

1.2.    3.

# Ants Marching

Words and Music by
David J. Matthews

The week ends, the week be-gins,_____ she__ thinks. We look at each
oth-er,___ won-d'ring what the oth - er is think - ing.___
But we nev-er say a____ thing_____ and these crimes be-tween
us grow deep-er. *Instrumental solo ad lib*

and re - mem - bers be - ing___ small, playing un - der the

ta - ble and dream - ing. Take___ these chanc - es,_____

place them in a___ box un - til___ a qui - et - er time. Lights___

___ down,- you up and die.___

*Play 3 times

(Sing 1st time only)
Instrumental solo ad lib

*On D. S. play 2 times.

red — and black an - ten - nae wav - ing. They all — do it the

same, they all — do it the same way, — yeah.

Can - dy man tempt - ing the thoughts of a

sweet tooth tor - tured, oh, by weight loss pro - gram, cut - ting the cor - ners,

*D.S. al Coda*

loose end, loose end, cut,– cut. On the fence could not– to of-fend, cut, cut,– cut, cut.

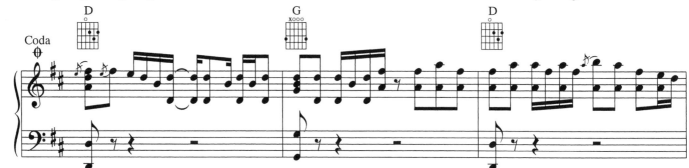

Coda

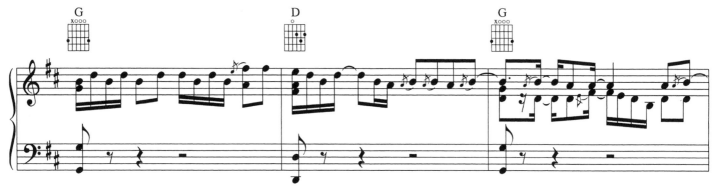

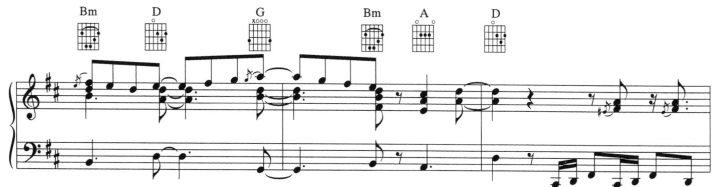

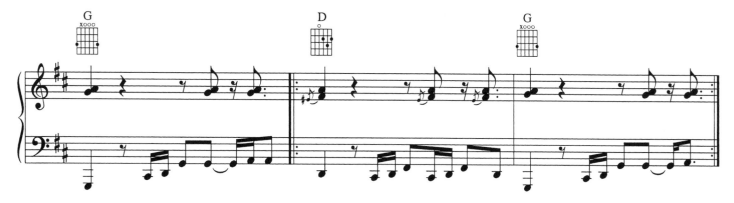

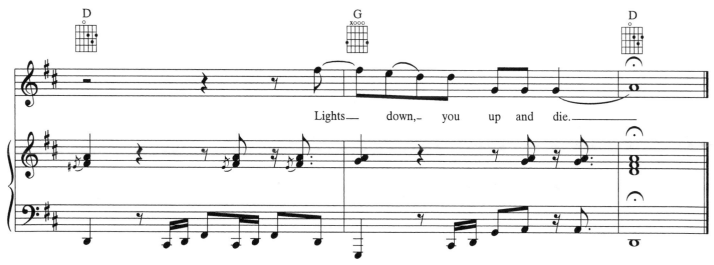

Lights— down,— you up and die._____

# The Best of What's Around

Words and Music by
David J. Matthews

**Moderate Rock**

1. Hey,— my friend,——————— it seems— your eyes— are trou-bled.
2. *See additional lyrics*

Care to— share—— your time— with— me?———

Would you say— you're feel - ing— low? And— so— a good—

noth - ing can be done,_____ we'll make the best of what's a - round._____

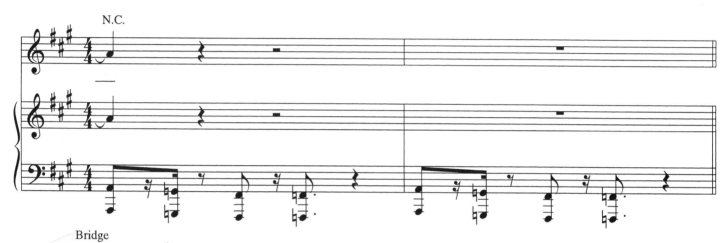

N.C.

Bridge

Turns out_____ not where,_____ but { 1.3. who you're with_____ that a - real - ly mat-
2. what you think_____ a - that } 

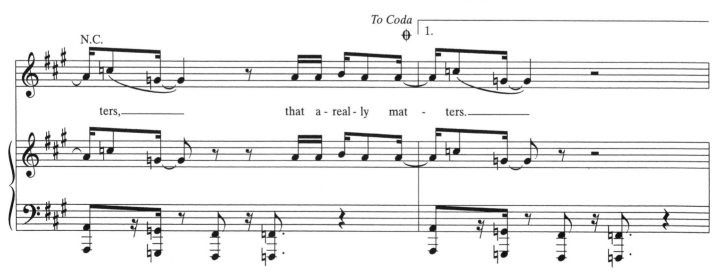

N.C.

*To Coda* ⊕ 1.

ters,_____ that a - real - ly mat - ters._____

And hurts_____ not much_____ when you're_____ a - round,_____

_____ when you're a - round._____ 2. And if_ you

ters,_____ that a - real-ly mat - ters,_____ that a - real-ly mat -

ters,_____ yeah.

*Additional Lyrics*

2. And if you hold on tight to what you think is your thing,
   You may find you're missing all the rest.
   Well, she run up into the light surprised.
   Her arms are open. Her mind's eye is...

*2nd Chorus:*
Seeing things from a better side than most can dream.
On a clearer road I feel, oh, you could say she's safe.
Whatever tears at her, whatever holds her down.
And if nothing can be done, she'll make the best of what's around. *(To Bridge)*

# Crash into Me

Words and Music by
David J. Matthews

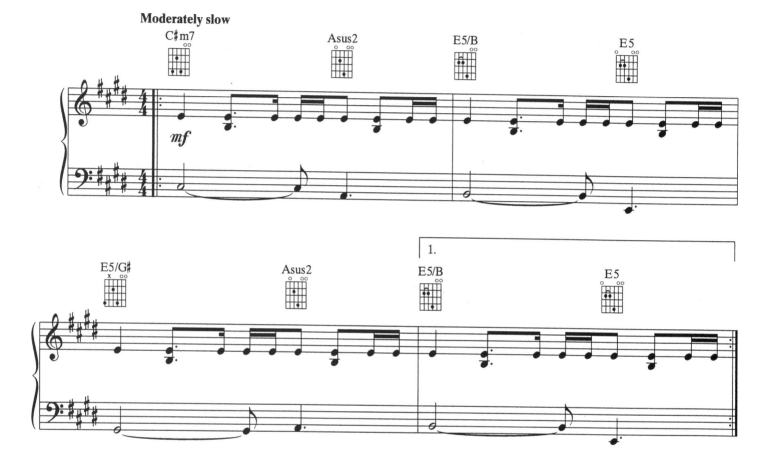

1. You've— got your ball,— you've got your chain——— tied—

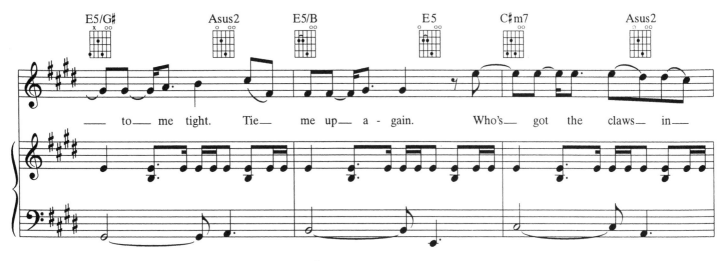

to — me tight. Tie — me up a - gain. Who's — got the claws — in —

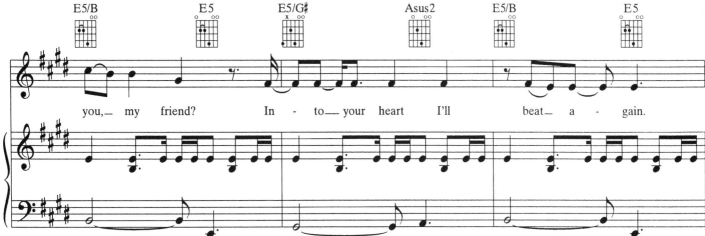

you, — my friend? In - to your heart I'll beat — a - gain.

Sweet — like can - dy to — — my — soul. Sweet — you rock and — —

— sweet — you — roll. — Lost — for you, I'm so — — lost — —

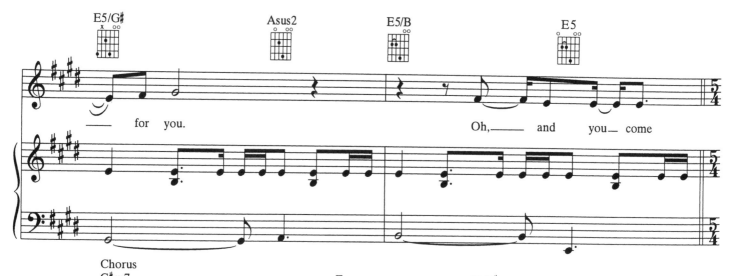

for you.

Oh,___ and you___ come

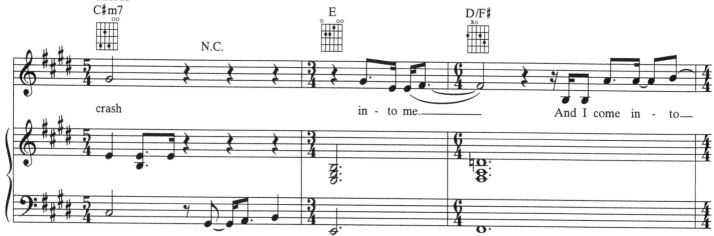

Chorus

crash

in - to me.___

And I come in - to___

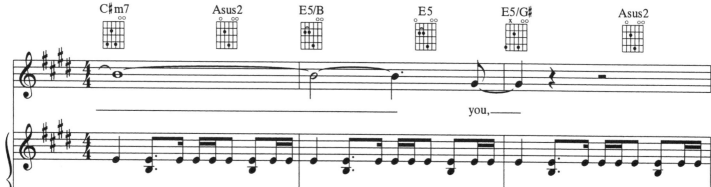

you,___

and I come in - to you.___

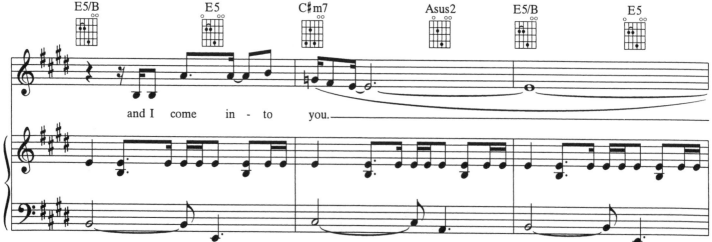

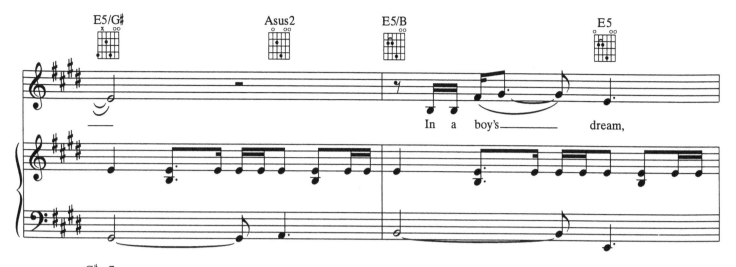

In a boy's___ dream,

in a boy's___

___ dream.

2. Touch your lips just so I know.
3. *See additional lyrics*

In your eyes, love, it glows so. I'm

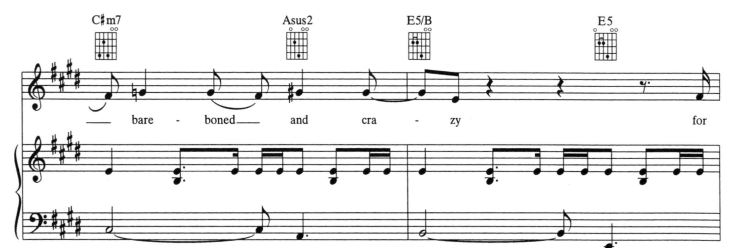

bare - boned and cra - zy for you.

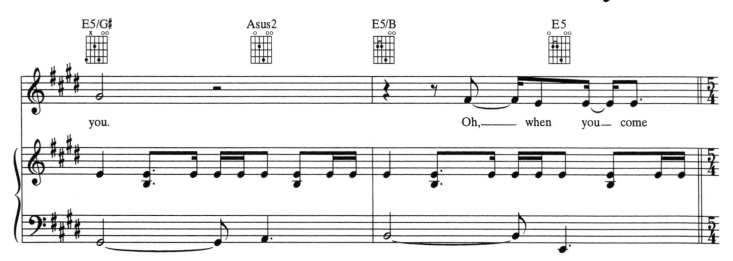

you. Oh, when you come

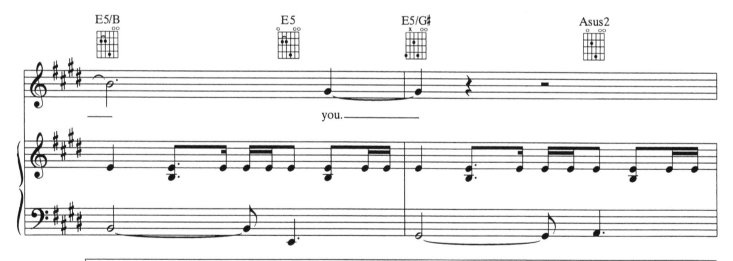

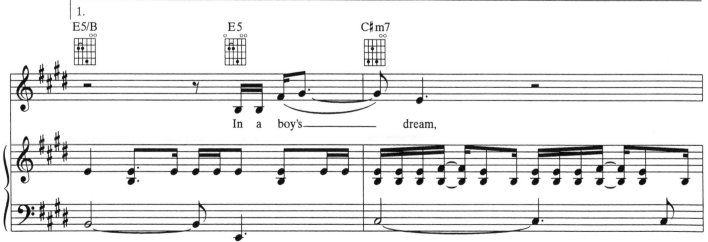

in a boy's dream.

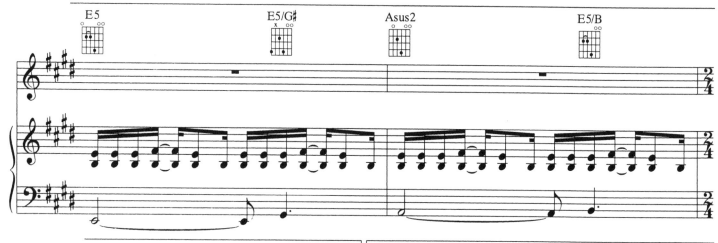

Oh,

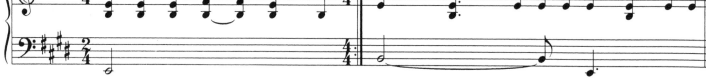

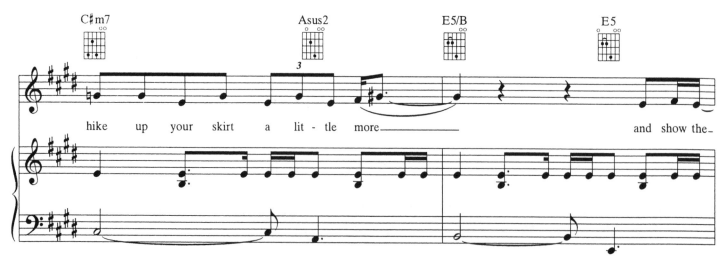

hike up your skirt a lit-tle more and show the

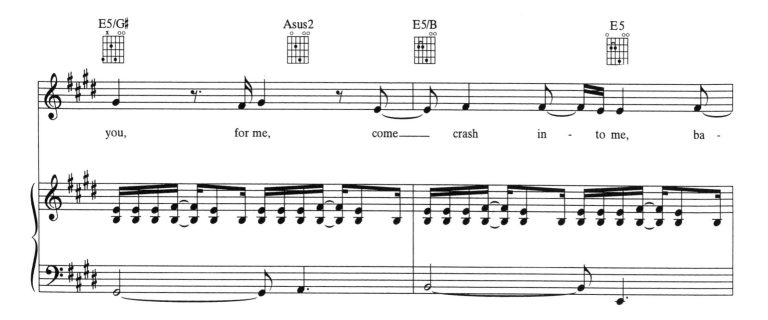

you, for me, come crash in - to me, ba -

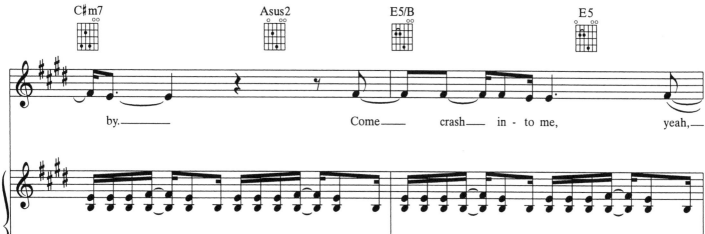

by. Come crash in - to me, yeah,

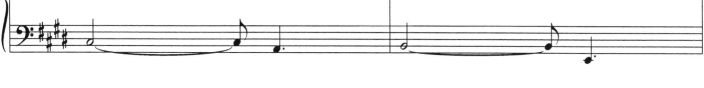

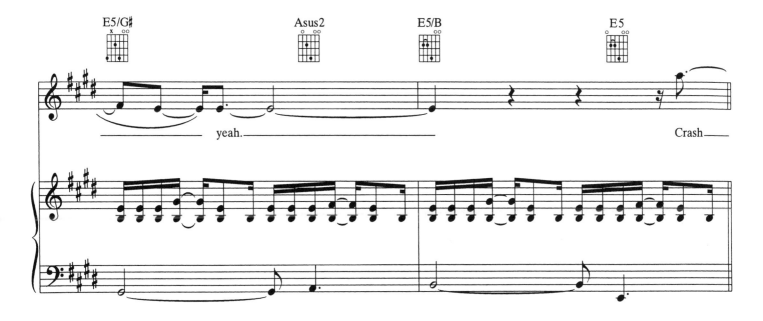

yeah. Crash

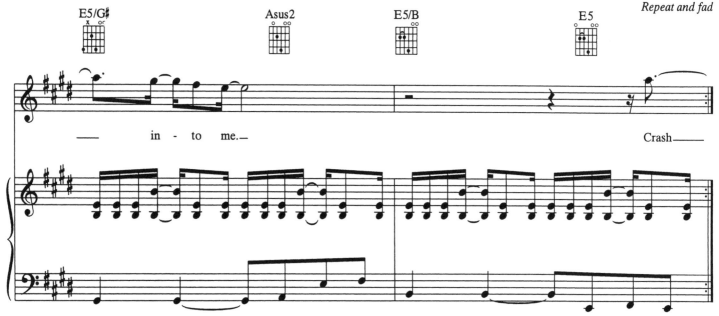

*Additional Lyrics*

3. Only if I've gone overboard,
   Then I'm begging you
   To forgive me, oh,
   In my haste.
   When I'm holding you so, girl,
   Close to me.
   Oh, and you come... *(To Chorus)*

# Crush

Words and Music by
David J. Matthews

Cra - zy           how  it

feels__ to - night.__ Cra - zy__ how__ you__ make it all al - right,_____ love.__ Crush__ me__ with__ the__ things__ you__ do.__ And I__ __ do__ for__ you__ an - y - thing__ too,_____ oh.__

And I won - der_____ this:_____ Could to - mor - row
Ly - ing un - der_____ this_____ spell you cast___ on
And it's times___ like_____ these_____ when my faith___ I

be_____ so___ won - drous as you there
me,_____ each___ mo - ment, the more I
feel_____ and___ I___ know how I

sleep - ing? Let's go_____ drive___ till
love you. Crush___ me,___ come___ on.
love you. Come___ on,___ come___ on,

*Play 1st time only*

morn - ing___ comes,___ watch___ the___ sun - rise___

36

To Coda

danc - ing on——— the ground.— Am I— right— side up or— up - side down?—

And is—— this real——————— or am I dream-ing?
Is this— real, oh,——————— or

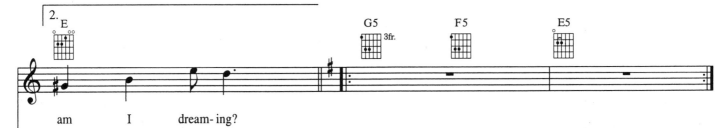

am I dream-ing?

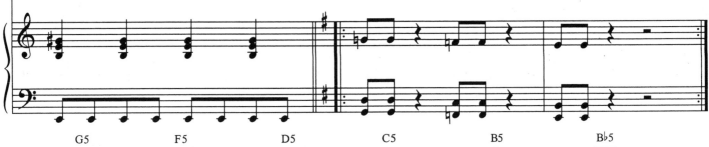

mean- ing I'll— hold— you. But please,——— please,— just let me

al - ways...

# Dancing Nancies

Words and Music by
David J. Matthews

Could I have been your little broth-

er? Could I have been, oh, an-y-one oth-er than

me? Could I have been, oh, an-y-one oth-er than

me? Could I have been an-y-one oth-er than

**Moderately fast**

44

an - y - one oth - er____ than____ me? And then I

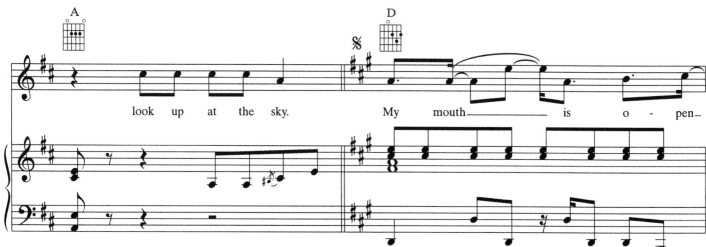

look up at the sky. My mouth____ is o - pen____

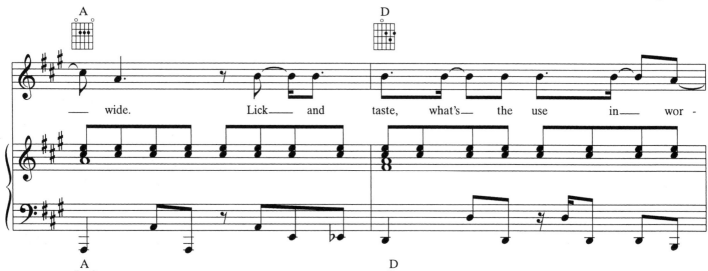

____ wide. Lick____ and taste, what's____ the use in____ wor -

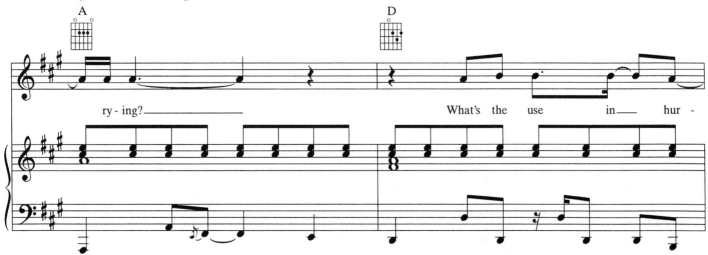

ry - ing?____ What's the use in____ hur -

ry- ing?_____ Turn,_____ turn, we al - most be-come diz -

*3rd time to Coda II*         *2nd time to Coda I*

*Play 4 times*

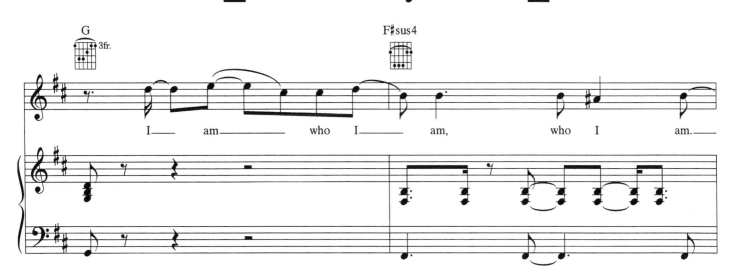

zy. *(Sing 1st time only)*

I___ am____ who I____ am, who I am.___

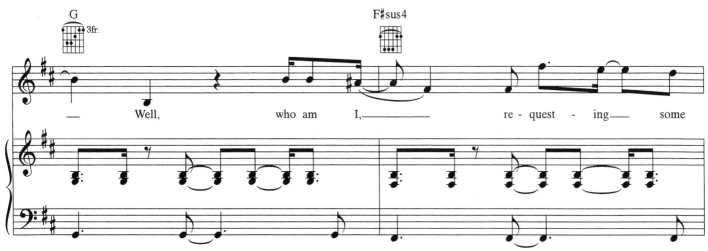

___ Well, who am I,_____ re - quest - ing___ some

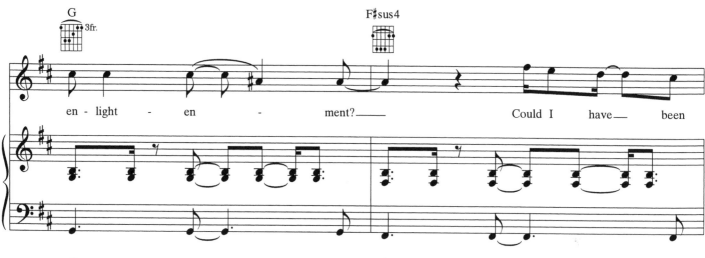

en - light - en - ment?\_\_\_ Could I have\_\_\_ been

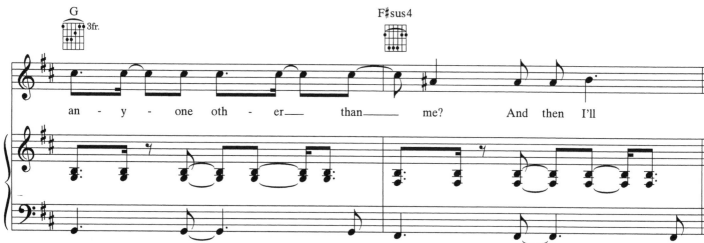

an - y - one oth - er\_\_\_ than\_\_\_ me? And then I'll

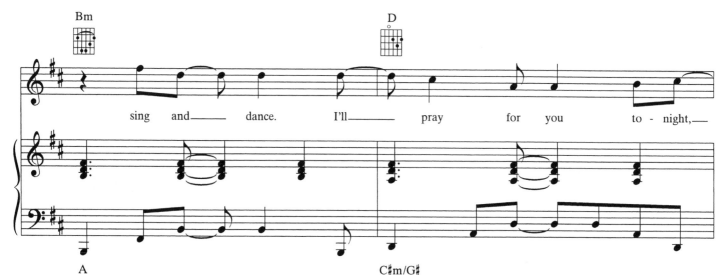

sing and\_\_\_ dance. I'll\_\_\_ pray for you to - night,\_\_\_

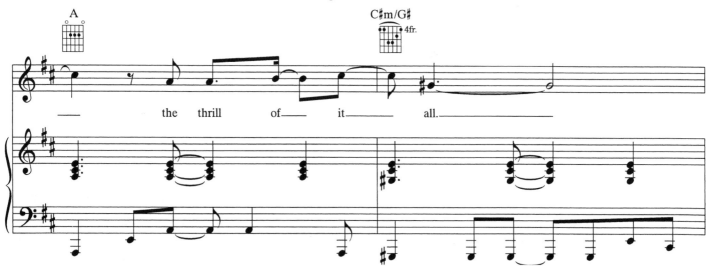

\_\_\_ the thrill of\_\_\_ it\_\_\_ all._____

# Digging a Ditch

Lyrics by David J. Matthews

Music by Dave Matthews Band

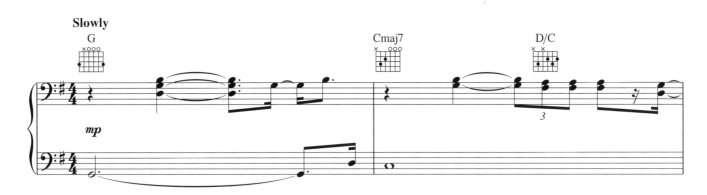

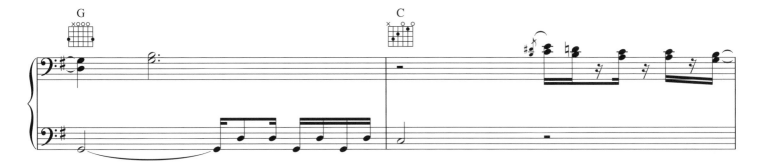

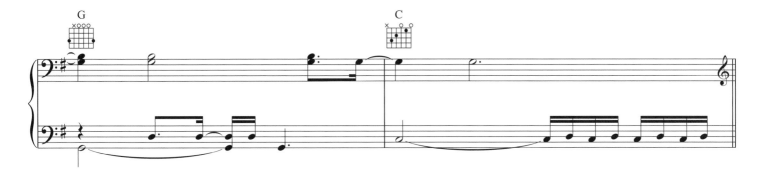

Run __ to your dream - ing ___ when ___ you're a - lone.

Un - plug the T - V ___ and turn off your phone.

Get ___ heav - y on with ___ dig - ging your ___ ditch. ___ 'Cause I'm ___

___ dig - ging a ___ ditch where ___ mad - ness ___ gives a bit.

Dig - ging a ___ ditch where si - lence ___ lives. ___

55

these \_\_\_\_ ques - tions spin - ning a - round my \_\_\_ head \_\_\_ will die, \_\_\_

will die, \_\_\_

will die. \_\_\_

Run \_\_ to your dream - ing \_\_\_\_ when \_\_\_ you're a - lone.

56

*D.S. al Coda*

Un - plug the T - V __ and turn off your phone.

Get __ heav - y on with __ dig - ging your __ ditch. __ 'Cause I'm __

**Coda**

Where all __

__ these __ hab - its __ that pull heav - y at __ my heart __ will die. __

Run to your dream - ing ___ when you're a - lone.

Not ___ what you should be ___ or what ___ you've be - come. Just ___

___ get ___ heav - y on with ___ dig - ging your ___ ditch. ___ 'Cause I'm

dig - ging a ___ ditch where ___ mad - ness ___ gives a bit.

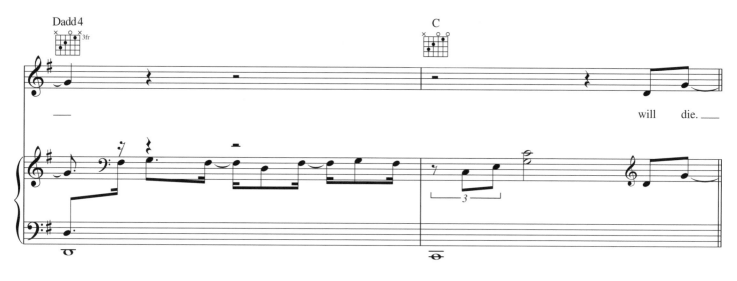

will die. ___

___ Run ___ to your dream - ing ___ when ___ you're a - lone.

Un - plug the T - V ___ and turn ___ off your phone.

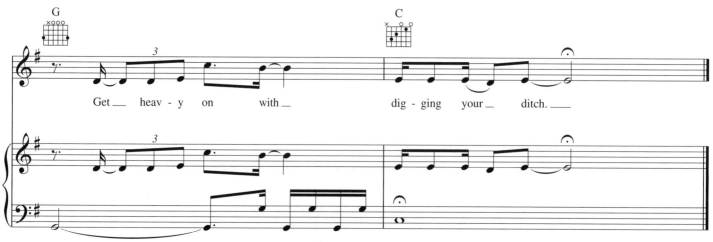

Get ___ heav - y on with ___ dig - ging your ___ ditch. ___

# Don't Drink the Water

Words and Music by
David J. Matthews

you not    see?

**D5**

There's no  place here. What were you ex - pect - ing?
A - way,  a - way, you have been ban - ished.
Here's the hitch... Your horse is leav - ing.

No room for both,  just  room for me.
Your land is gone  and  giv - en
Don't miss your boat,  it's  leav - ing

**G5**

— me.    So you will lay  your
me.    And here  I  will
now.    And as  you go  I will

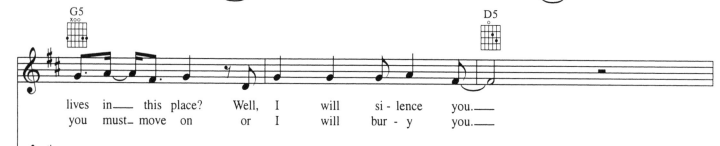

What's that___ you say?___ Your fa - ther's spir - it___ still
All I___ can say___ to you, my new neigh - bor,___ is

lives in___ this place? Well, I will si - lence you.___
you must_ move on or I will bur - y you.___

*To Coda*
⊕

*D.S. (no repeat) al Coda*
𝄋

64

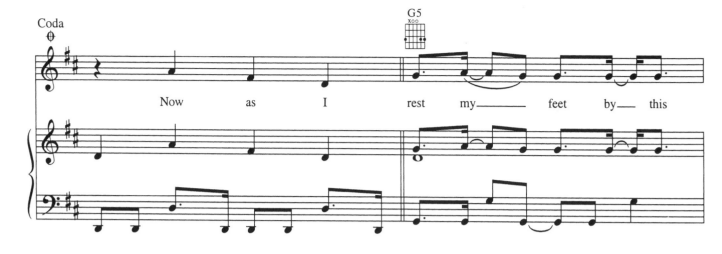

Coda

Now as I rest my feet by this

fi - re, those hands once warmed here, but I have re - tired

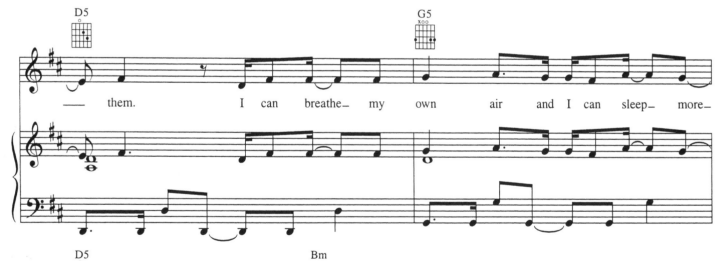

them. I can breathe my own air and I can sleep more

sound - ly. Up - on these poor souls I'll build

*Repeat and fade

*After fading out, continue to Interlude.

**Moderately**

Interlude

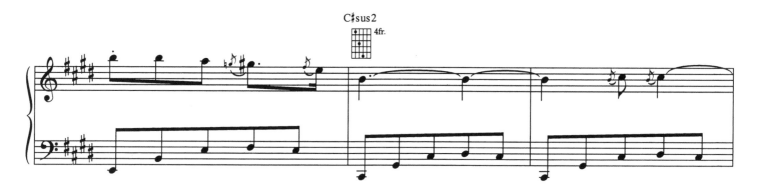

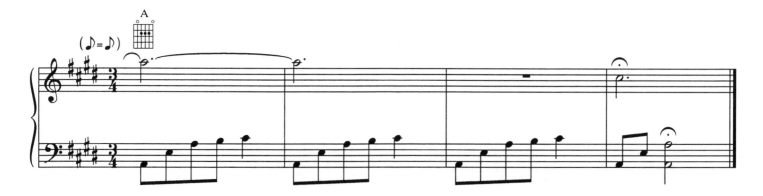

# The Dreaming Tree

Words and Music by
David J. Matthews and Stefan Lessard

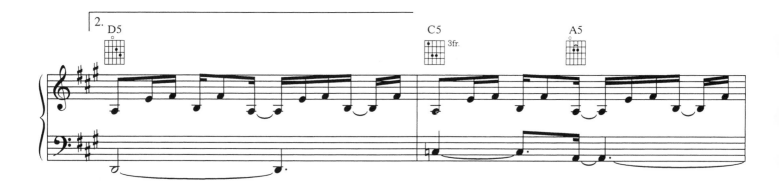

Stand - ing—
From— the—

here, the old— man said— to me, "Long be-fore— these crowd-ed
start, she knew— she had— it made. Eas - y up till

streets, here stood my dream-ing tree." Be-low— it he would
then, for sure— she'd make the grade. A - dor - ers came in

70

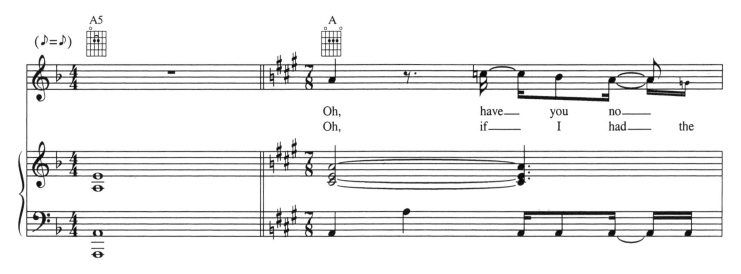

Oh,    have  you  no   the
Oh,    if   I  had  the

*Play 1st time only*

pit - y?    This  thing  I  do,  I  do  not  de -

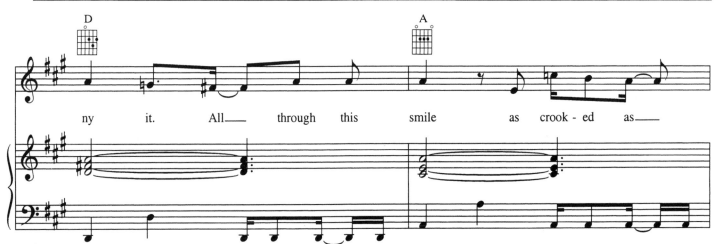

ny  it.  All  through  this  smile  as  crook - ed  as

dan - ger,  do  not  de - ny.  I  know  in

74

my mind I would leave you now. If I had the

strength to, I would leave you up to your own de-

vic - es. Will you not talk? Can you take pit - y? I don't ask

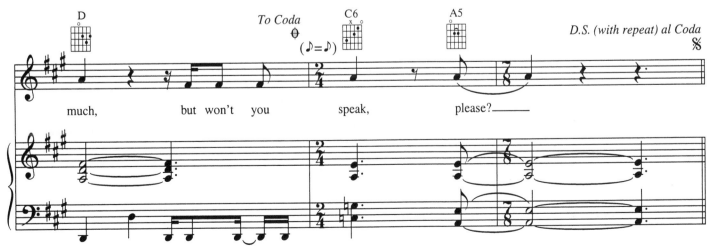

much, but won't you speak, please?

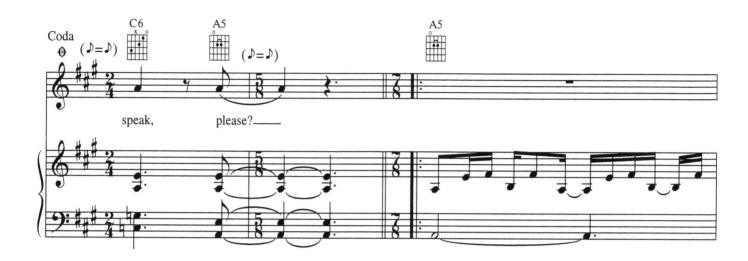

speak, please?

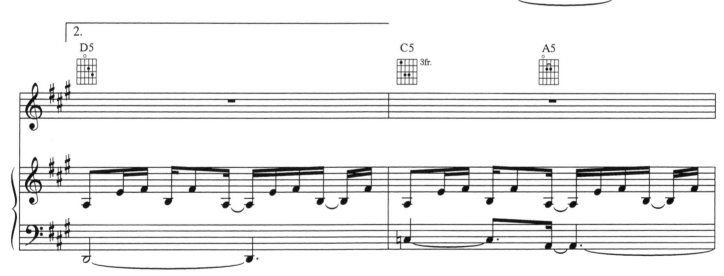

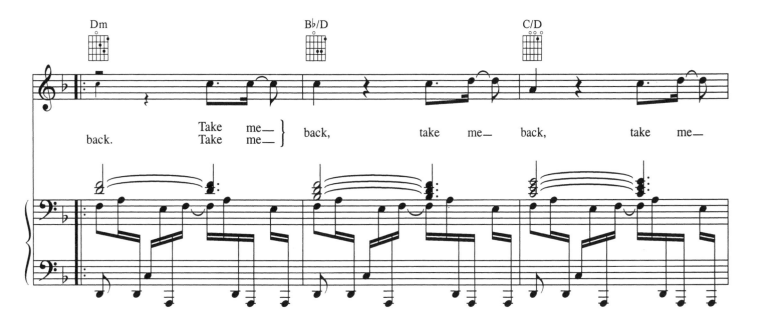

back.  Take me } back,  take me back,  take me

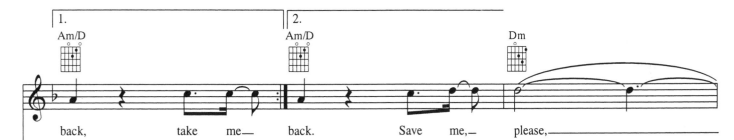

1.  back,  take me back.  2.  Save me, please,

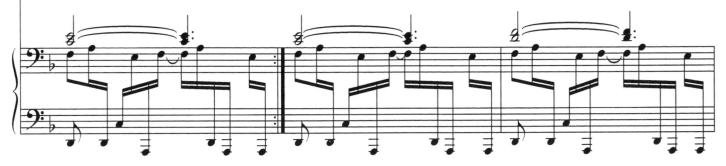

take me back.

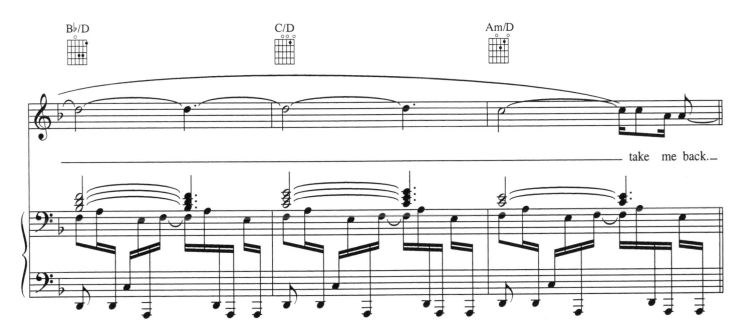

*(Sing 1st time only)*

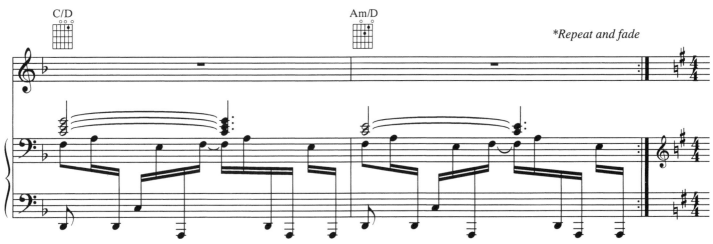

*\*Repeat and fade*

*\*After fading out,
continue to Interlude.*

**Moderately**

Interlude
N.C.

# Everybody Wake Up

## (Our Finest Hour Arrives)

Words and Music by
Dave Matthews Band and Mark Batson

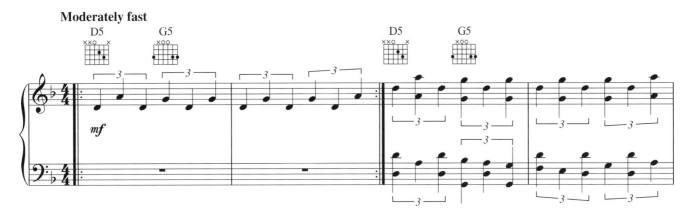

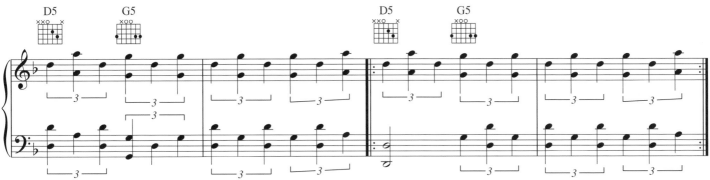

Ev - 'ry - bod - y wake up _____ if you're liv - ing with your eyes closed. _____

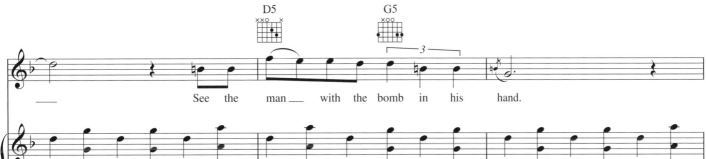

_____ See the man _____ with the bomb in his hand.

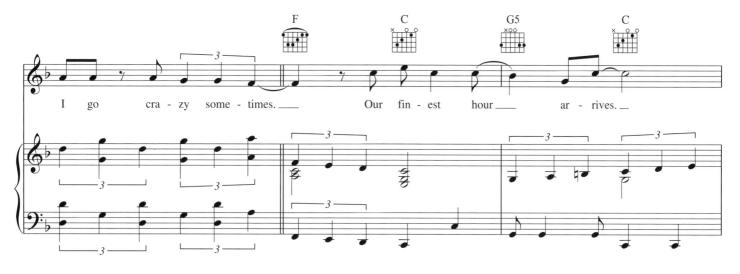

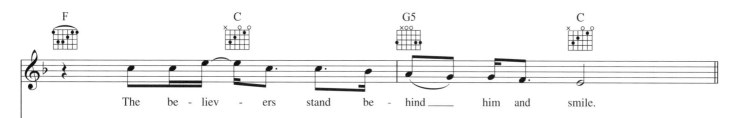

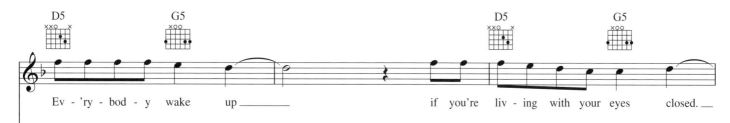

It just leaves a room __ full of blind men. _____ Our fin - est hour __

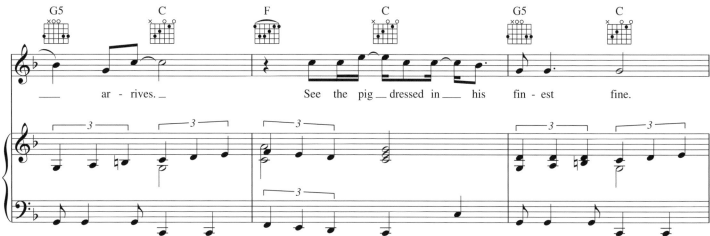

__ ar - rives. __ See the pig __ dressed in ___ his fin - est fine.

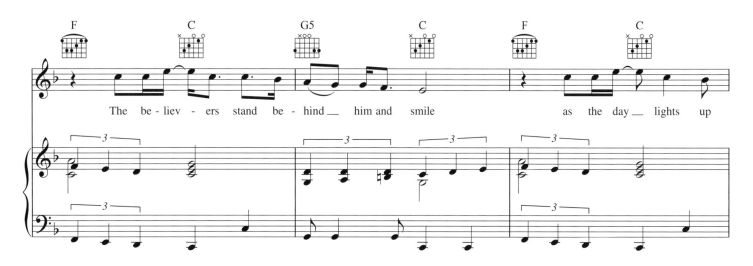

The be - liev - ers stand be - hind __ him and smile as the day __ lights up

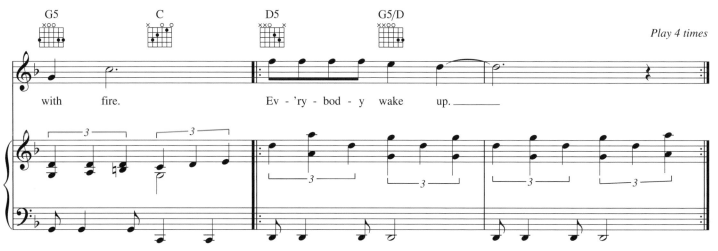

*Play 4 times*

with fire. Ev - 'ry - bod - y wake up. _____

83

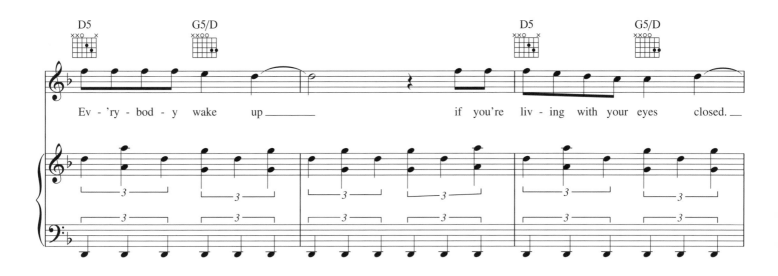

Ev - 'ry - bod - y wake up ____ if you're liv - ing with your eyes closed. __

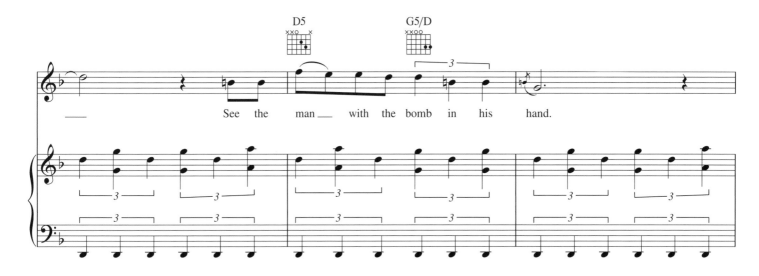

____ See the man ___ with the bomb in his hand.

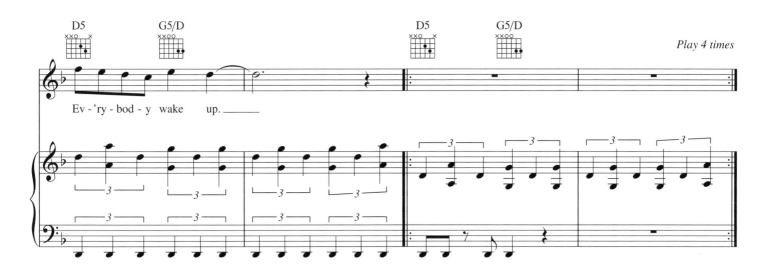

Ev - 'ry - bod - y wake up. _____

*Play 4 times*

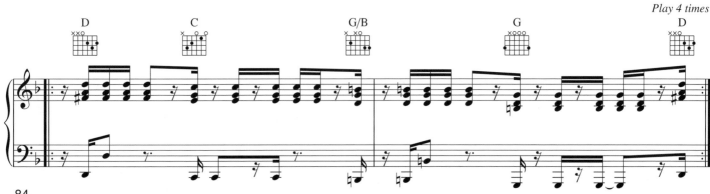

*Play 4 times*

# Everyday

Words and Music by
David J. Matthews and Glen Ballard

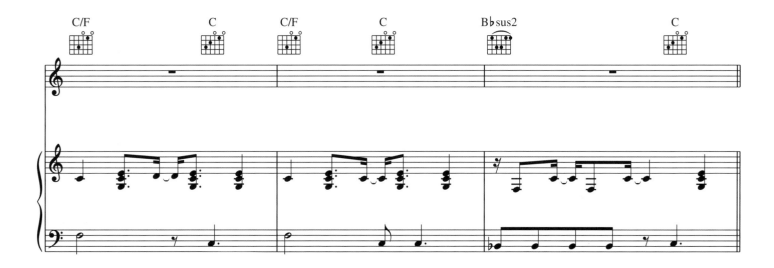

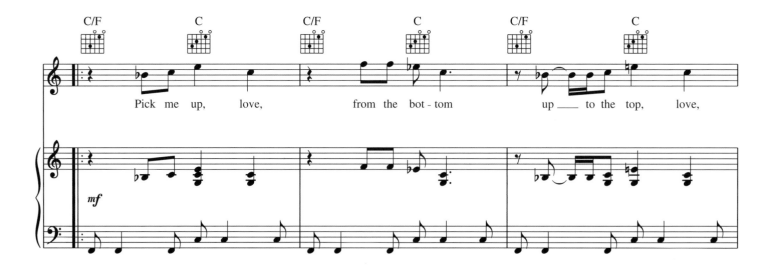

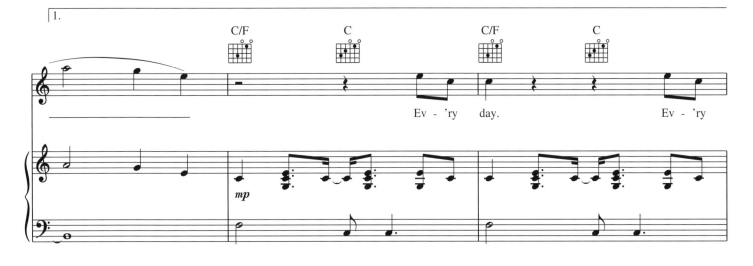

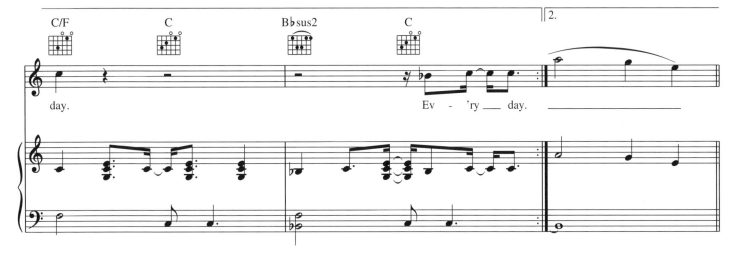

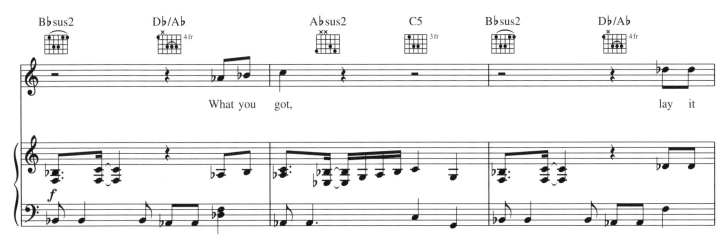

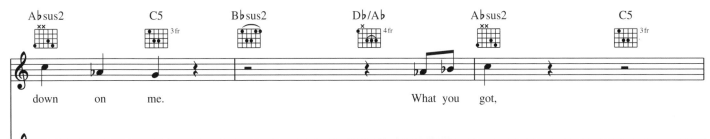

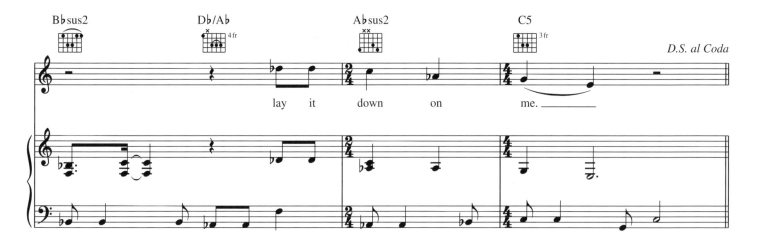

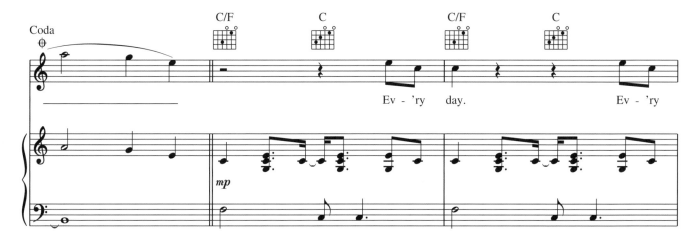

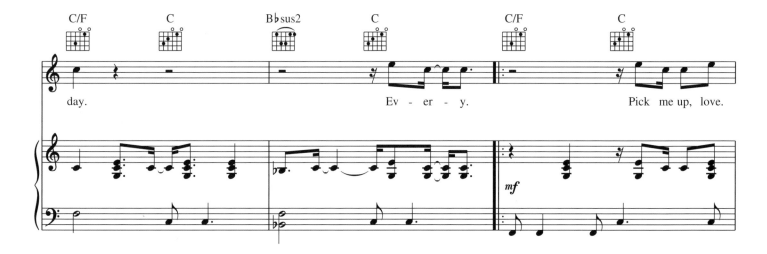

90

# Grace Is Gone

Lyrics by David J. Matthews

Music by Dave Matthews Band

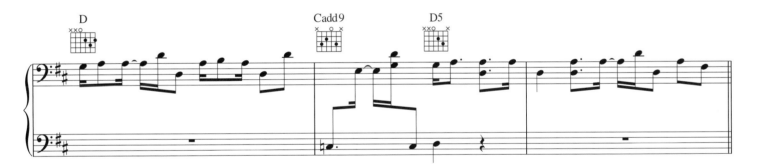

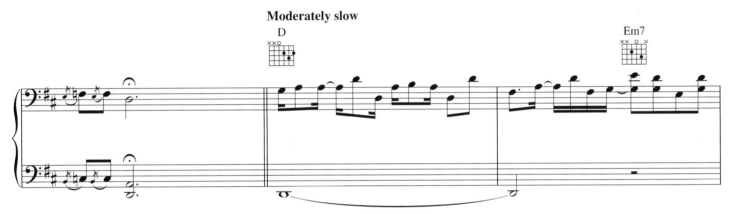

Ne - on shines _____ through smok - y eyes _____ to - night. _____ It's

two A. M., ___ I'm ___ drunk a - gain. It's heav - y on ___ my ___

___ mind. ___

I could nev - er love ___ a - gain so much ___ as I ___ love ___ you. ___

never a-gain__ they fall__ up-on the one I so_____ a - dore.__

Ex - cuse__ me,__ please, one more__ drink.

Could you make it strong?__ 'Cause I don't need to think.__ She__

broke my__ heart, my_____ Grace is_____ gone.

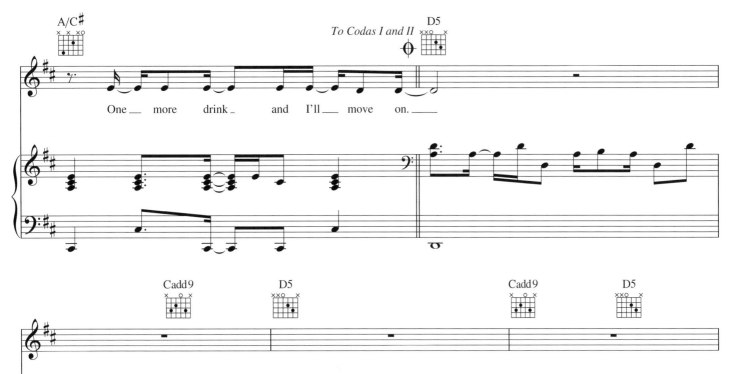

One — more drink — and I'll — move on. ___

One ___ drink to re - mem - ber, _____ then an -

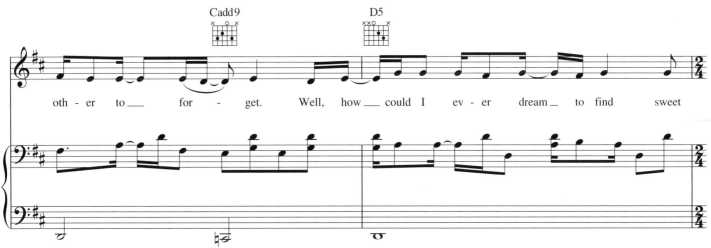

oth - er to ___ for - get. Well, how ___ could I ev - er dream_ to find sweet

love like you a-gain?___ One ___ drink to re- mem - ber and an- oth -

*D.S. al Coda I*

Coda I

er to ___ for - get. ___

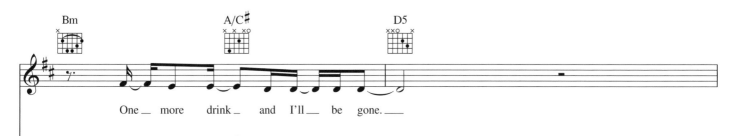

One ___ more drink ___ and I'll ___ be gone. ___

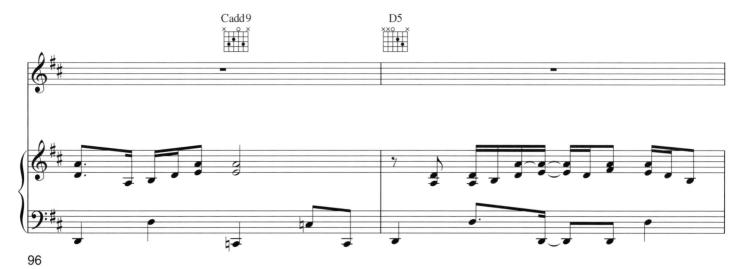

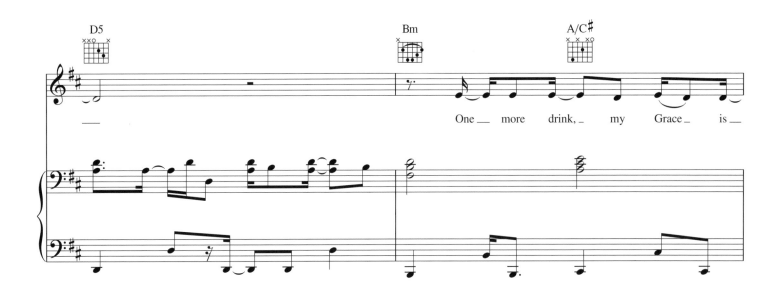

One — more drink, — my Grace — is —

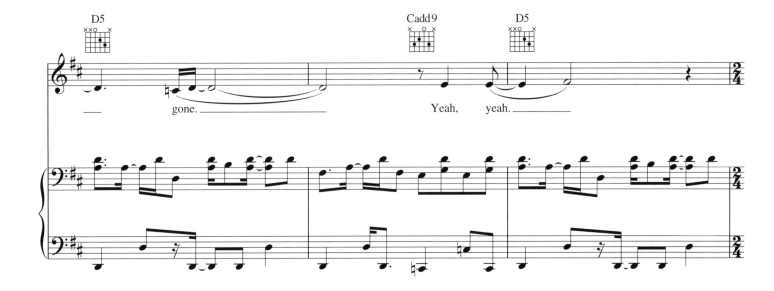

— gone. — Yeah, yeah. —

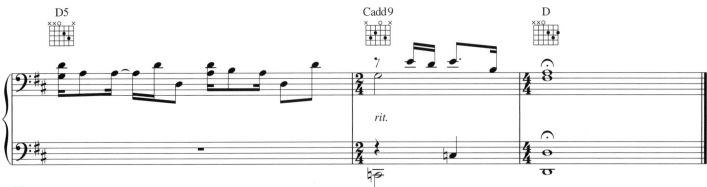

*rit.*

# Grey Street

Lyrics by David J. Matthews

Music by Dave Matthews Band

look at how ___ she lis - tens; she ___ says noth -
wish - es it ___ was dif - f'rent; she prays to God ___
stran - ger, speaks ___ out - side her door, says, ___ "Take what ___

ing of what she thinks. She just ___ goes
___ most of ev - 'ry night. And though ___ she
___ you can from your dreams. Make them ___ as

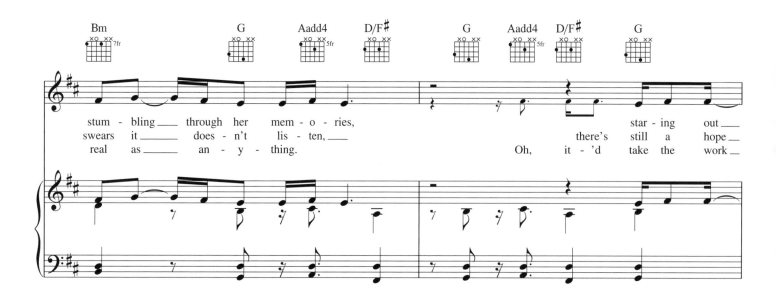

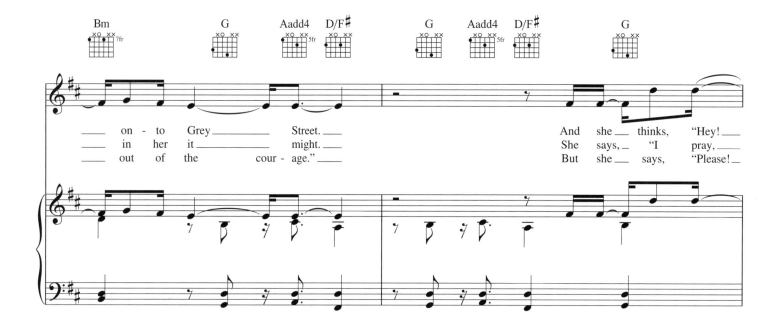

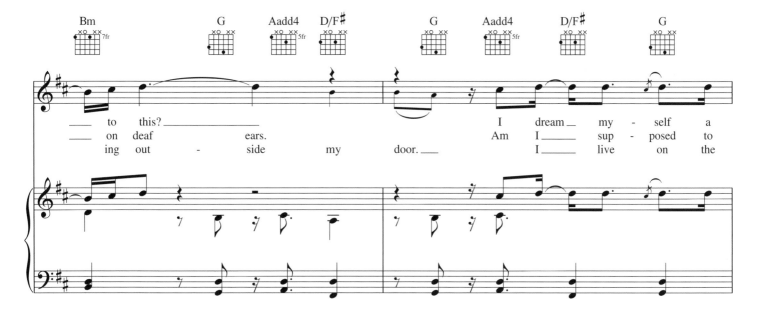

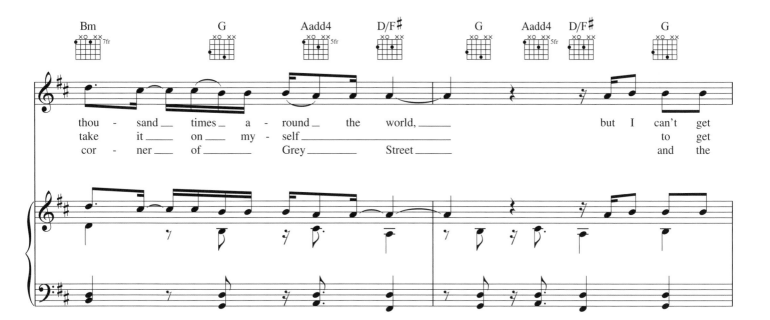

cold blue ice __ in __ her __ heart __ when all __ the col - ors __ mix to - geth -

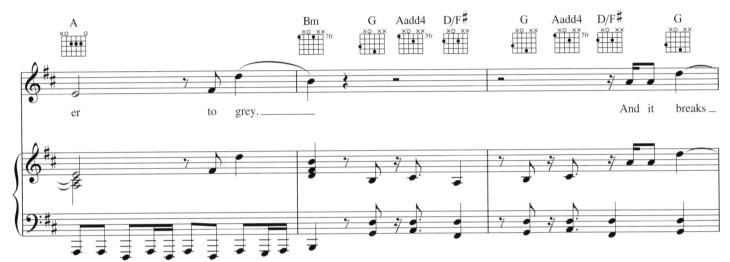

er __ to grey. _____ And it breaks __

*D.S. al Coda*

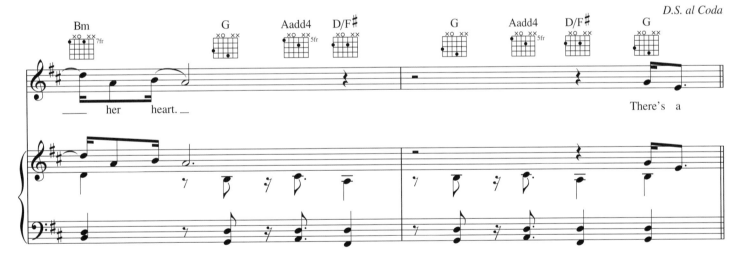

__ her heart. __ There's a

*Coda*

__ blood __ bleed - ing from her now, __ it's more like cold blue ice __ in her __

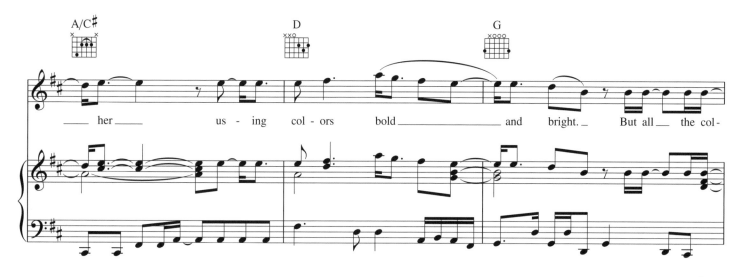

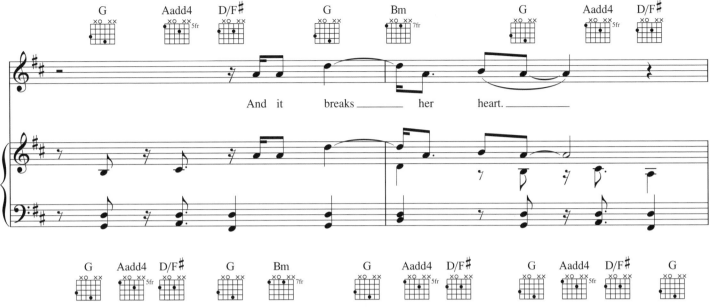

And it breaks _____ her heart. _____

Oh, it breaks _____ her heart _____ to grey. _____

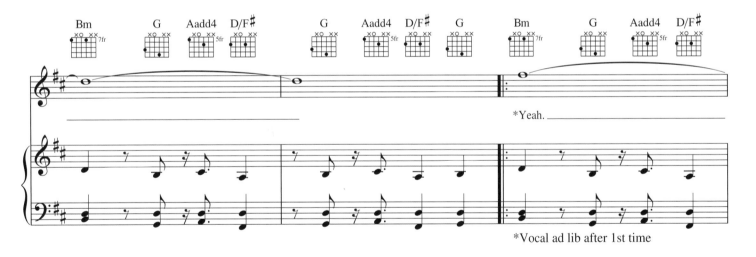

*Yeah. _____

*Vocal ad lib after 1st time

*Repeat and fade*

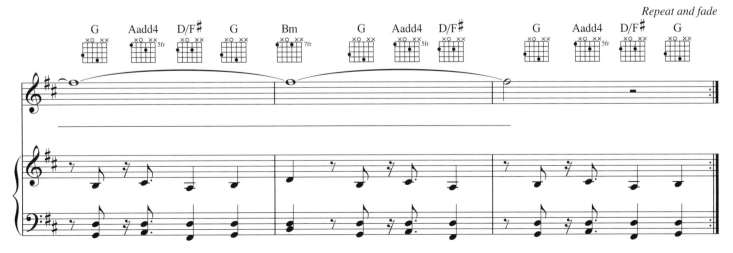

# Hunger For the Great Light

Words and Music by
Dave Matthews Band and Mark Batson

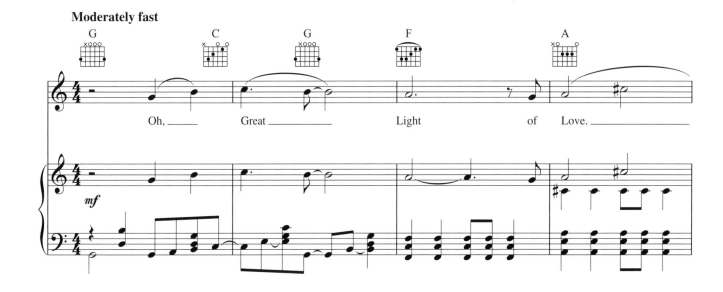

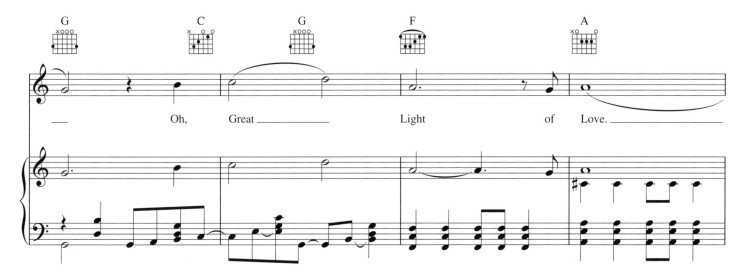

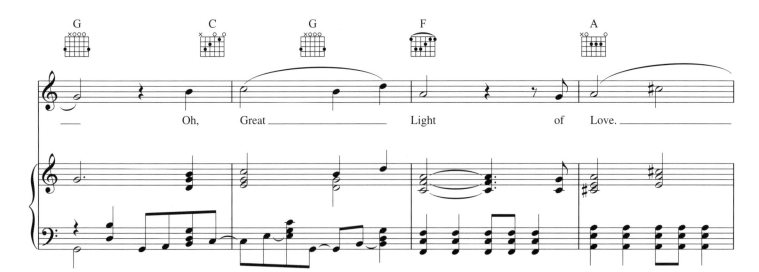

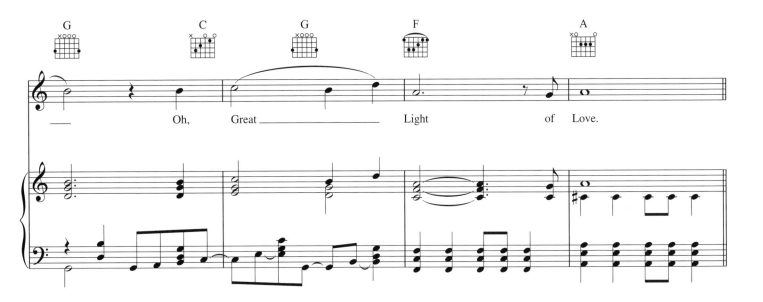

Oh,        Great _____ Light        of Love.

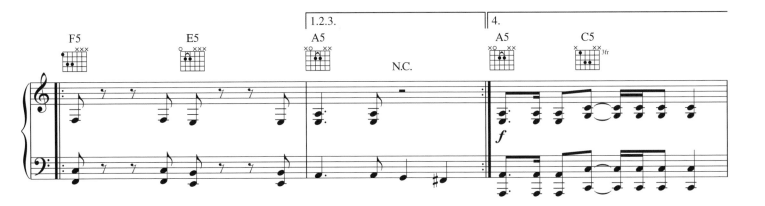

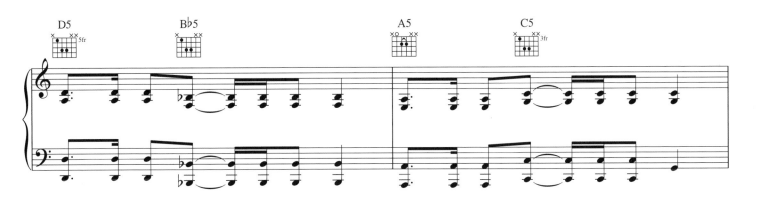

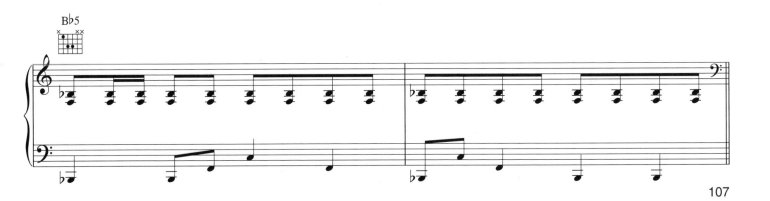

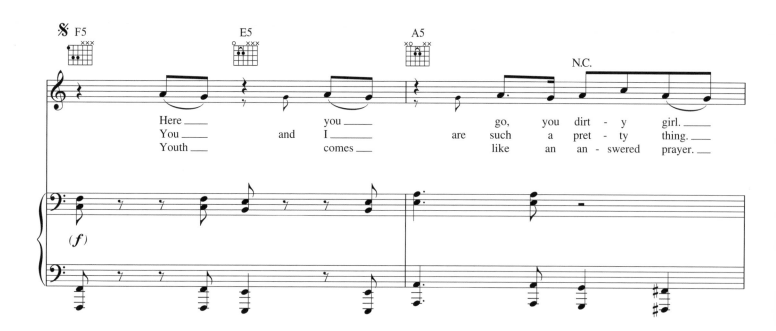

Here _____ you _____ go, you dirt - y girl. _____
You _____ and I _____ are such a pret - ty thing. _____
Youth _____ comes _____ like an an - swered prayer. _____

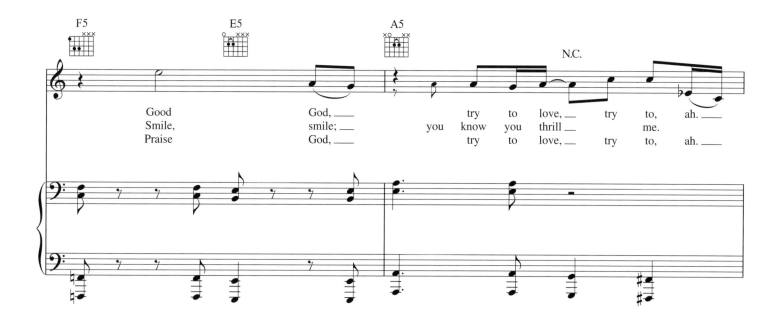

Good God, _____ try to love, _____ try to, ah. _____
Smile, smile; _____ you know you thrill _____ me.
Praise God, _____ try to love, _____ try to, ah. _____

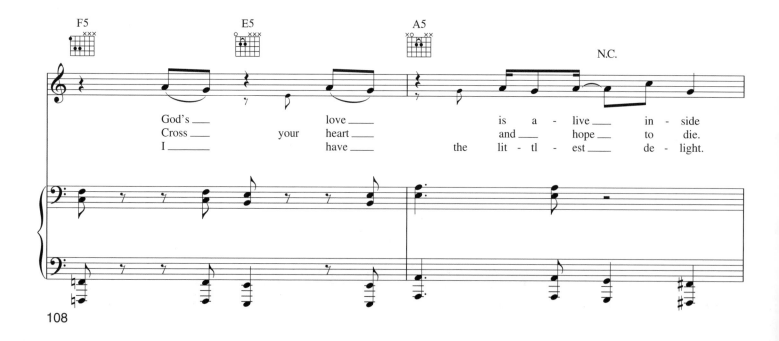

God's _____ love _____ is a - live _____ in - side
Cross _____ your heart _____ and _____ hope _____ to die.
I _____ have _____ the lit - tl - est _____ de - light.

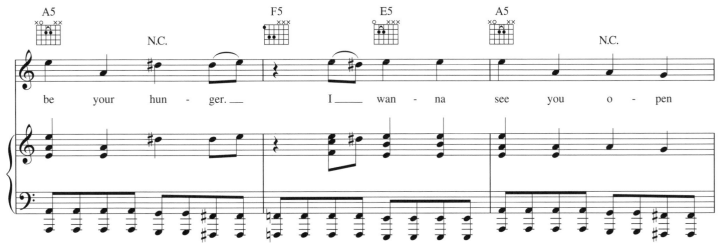

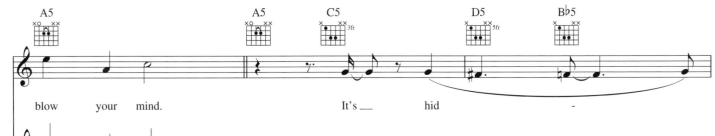

ing        to    cure _____ you.        My

*D.S. al Coda I*

aim, _____ to  love    you. _____ Huh.

**Coda I**

blow   your   mind.        You \_\_  and  I, \_\_\_   oh, \_\_\_   oh, \_\_\_

shine, \_    shine. \_        Oh,   Great _____

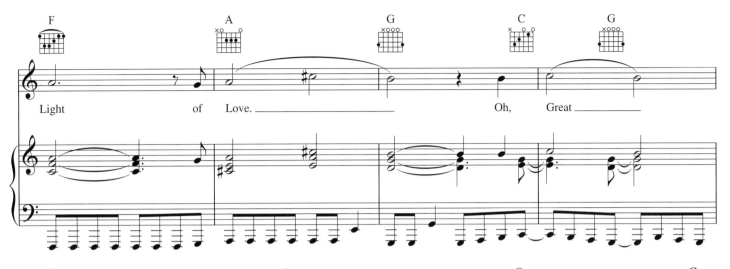

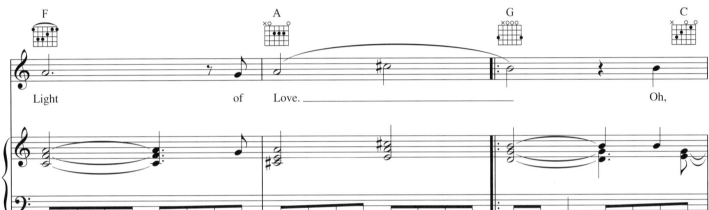

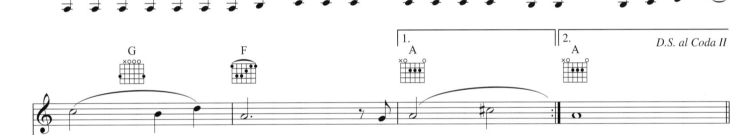

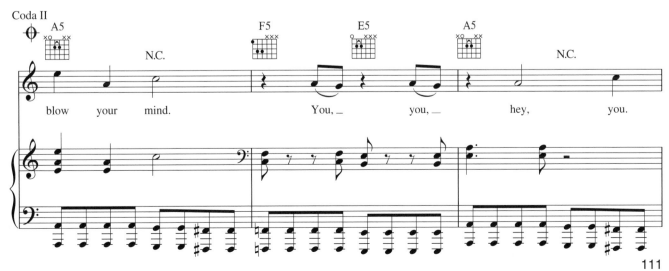

111

You, — you, — nah. — You, — you, —

oh.

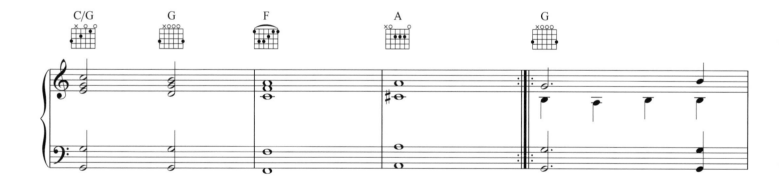

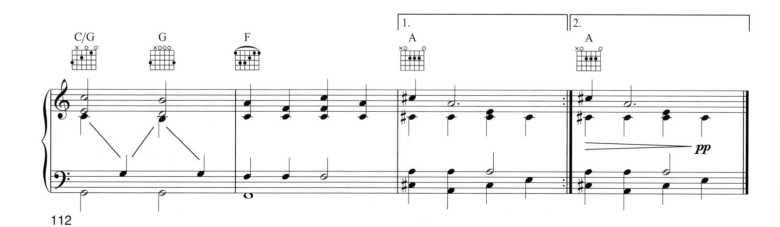

# I Did It

Words and Music by
David J. Matthews and Glen Ballard

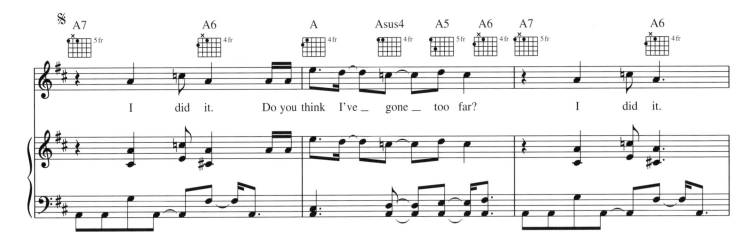

I did it. Do you think I've __ gone __ too far? I did it.

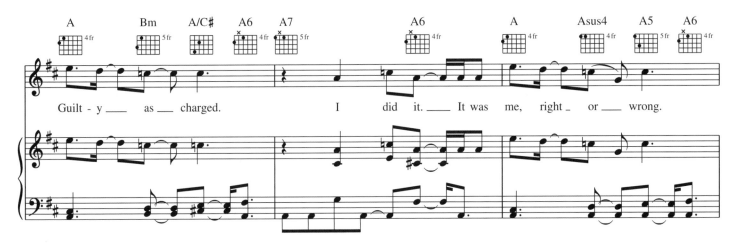

Guilt - y __ as __ charged. I did it. __ It was me, right __ or __ wrong.

*To Coda I*

I did it. Yeah. ___

I nev - er did a sin - gle thing that did a sin - gle thing to change __ the ug - ly ways of the world.

114

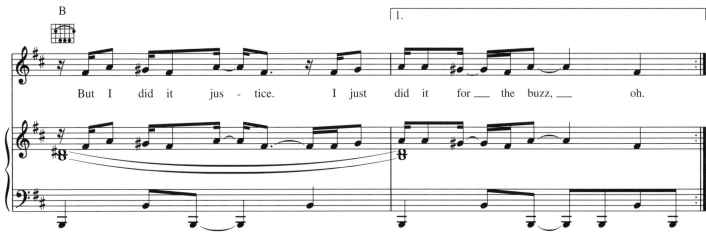

117

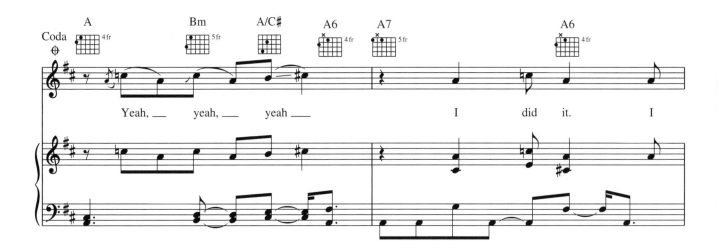

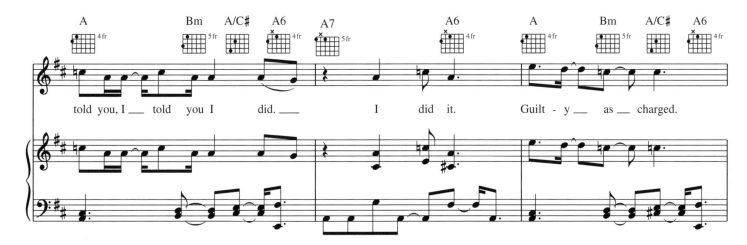

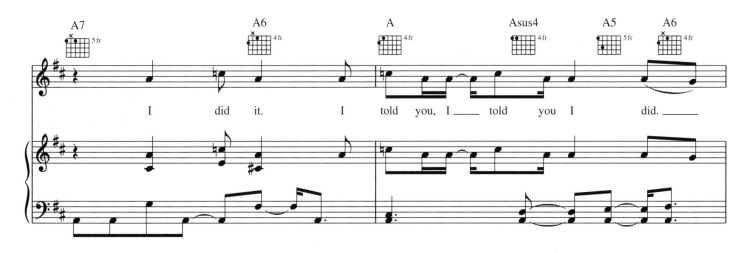

*D.S.S. (take 2nd ending) al Fine*

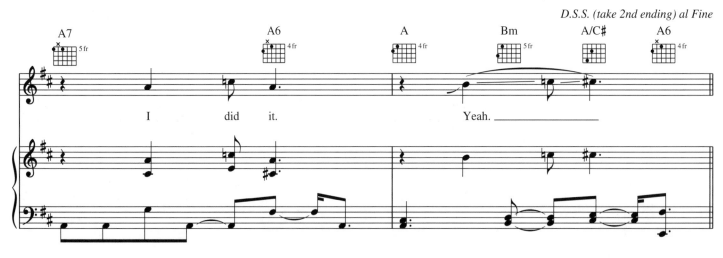

# Jimi Thing

Words and Music by
David J. Matthews

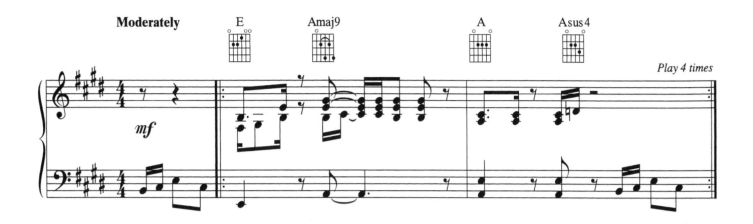

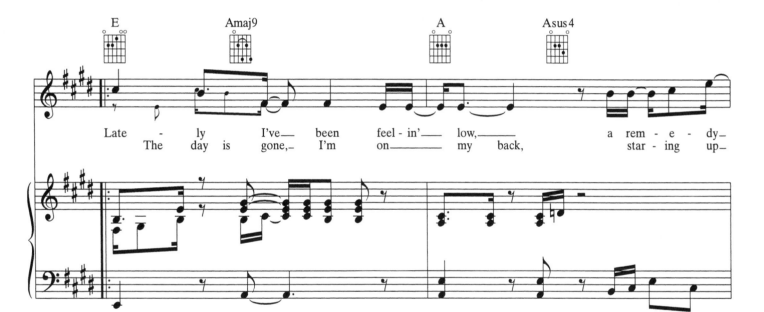

Late - ly I've - been feel - in' low, a rem - e - dy
The day is gone, I'm on my back,

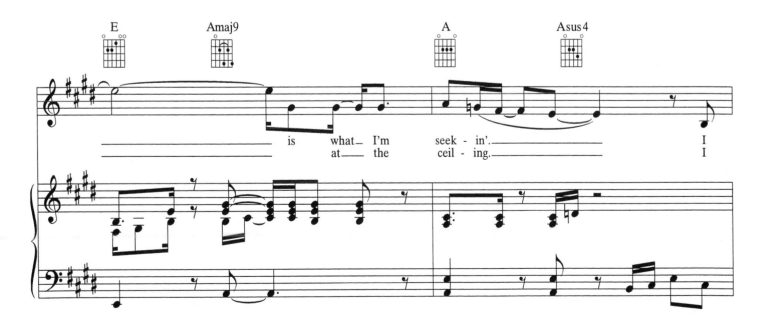

is what I'm seek - in'. I
at the ceil - ing. I

ing          just for a while,_____          I'll get___ back          to___ you._____

_____

1. Some - times          a          Jim - i___ thing
2.3. Some - times___ I take a Jim - i          thing,_____

slides          in my way          keep          me          swing - in'.     I'd          like          to show___
_____ just          keep          me          swing - in'.

___ you          what's___ in - side,_____          but I          should - n't          care_____

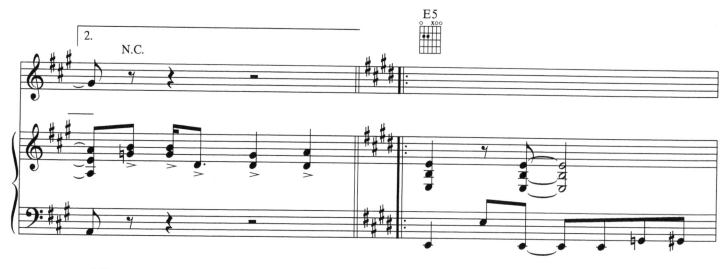

Late - ly I've_____

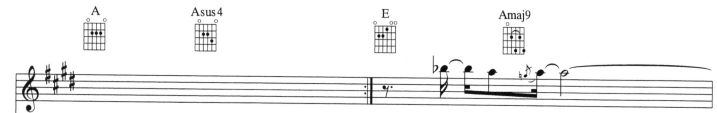

____ been feel - in' low._____ Well, the rem - e - dy is___ what I'm look - in'

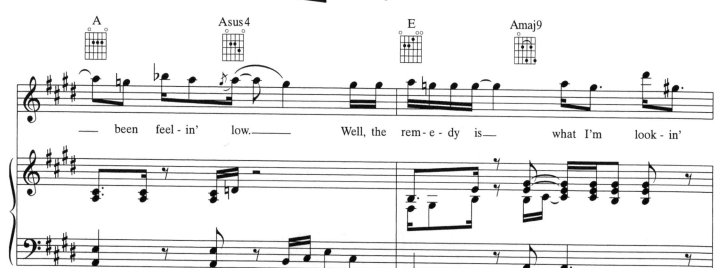

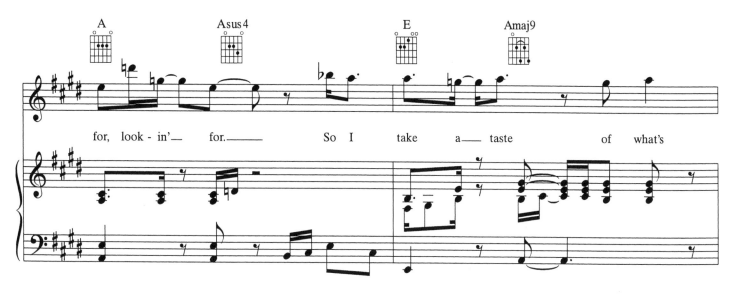

for, look-in'— for._____ So I take a— taste of what's

be-low._____ Come a-way._____

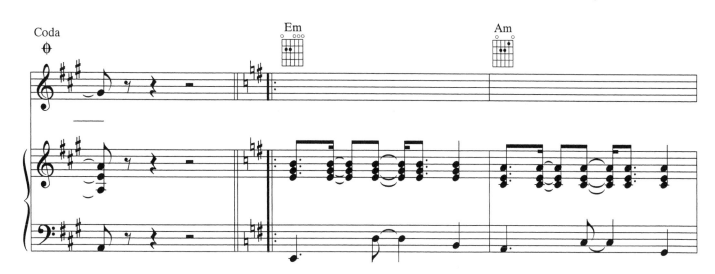

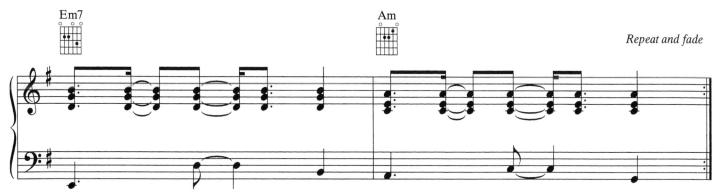

# Louisiana Bayou

Words and Music by
Dave Matthews Band and Mark Batson

**Moderately**

No, no, Ma-ma cried dev - il; they do - si - do.
Sweet girl, Dad-dy done beat that girl like he's in - sane.
Mon-ey on my bed, but you ain't got to go.

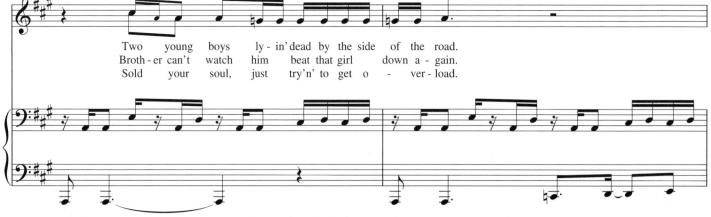

Two young boys ly - in' dead by the side of the road.
Broth - er can't watch him beat that girl down a - gain.
Sold your soul, just try'n' to get o - ver - load.

bay - ou,    try'n' to play with the cane,  you,    ah.    Try'n' to play with with cane, 
bay - ou.)

    you,    ah.    Same sto - ry a - gain,  you,    ah.   
(Lou - i - si - an - a

Bay - ou.
bay - ou.)

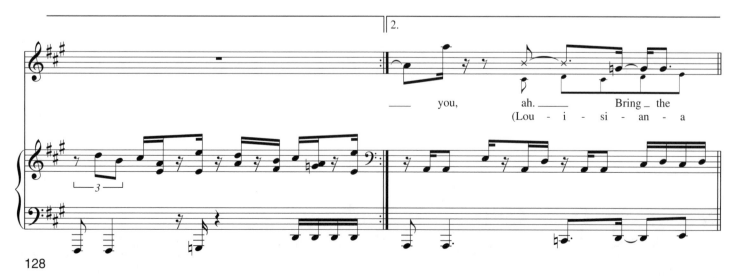

    you,    ah.    Bring  the
(Lou - i - si - an - a

same. No, no. Ma - ma cried dev - il; they do - si - do.
bay - ou.)

See two young boys ly - in' dead by the side of the road. Shame, _

shame. Oh, it's a shame to lose your way _ run - ning _

_ wild. It's a shame _ to lose your... Shame,

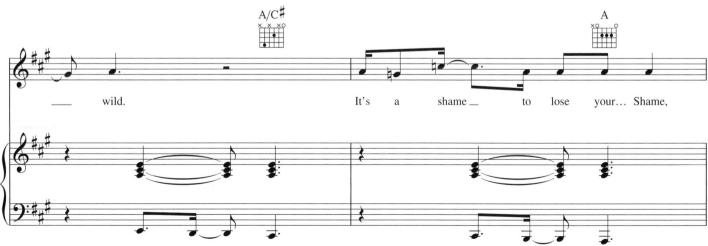

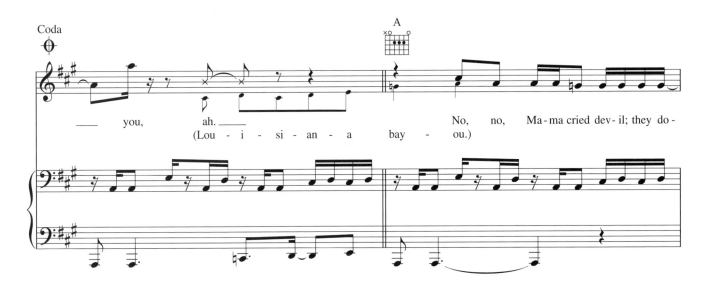

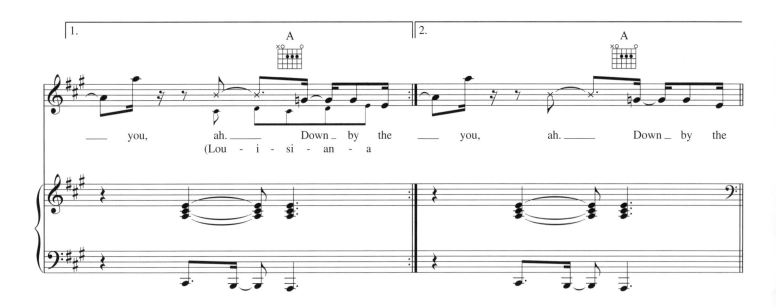

you, ah. _____ Down_ by the _____ you, ah. _____ Down_ by the
(Lou - i - si - an - a

bay - ou,

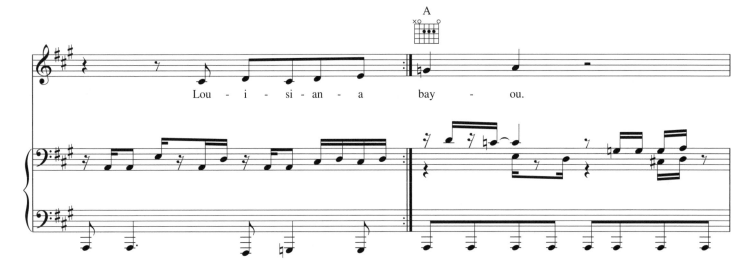

Lou - i - si - an - a bay - ou.

*Repeat and fade*

# Out of My Hands

Words and Music by
Dave Matthews Band and Mark Batson

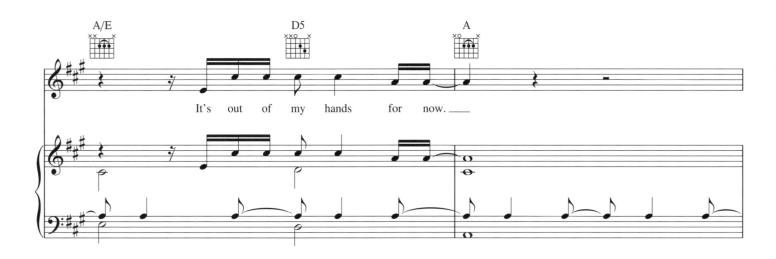

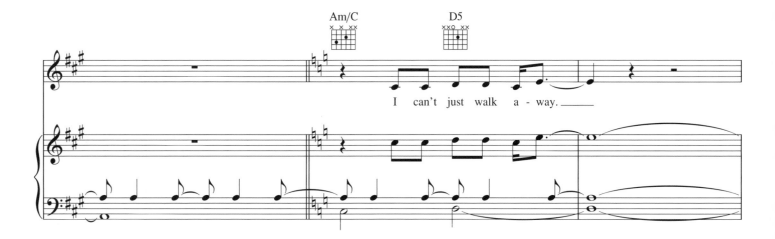

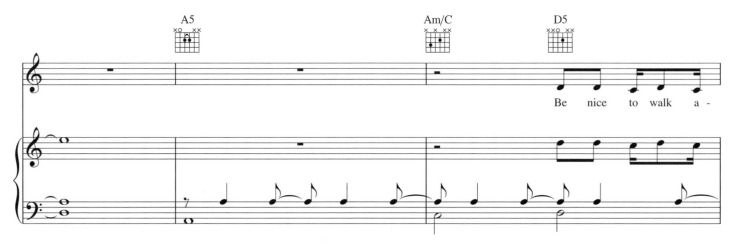

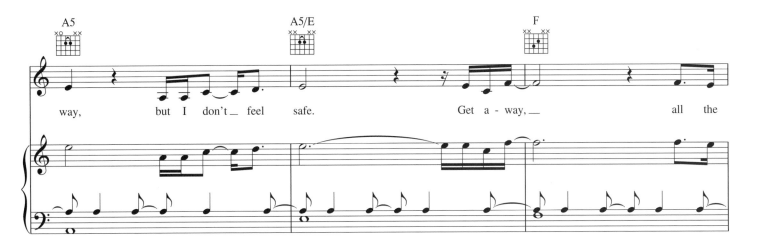

way, but I don't ___ feel safe. Get a - way, ___ all the

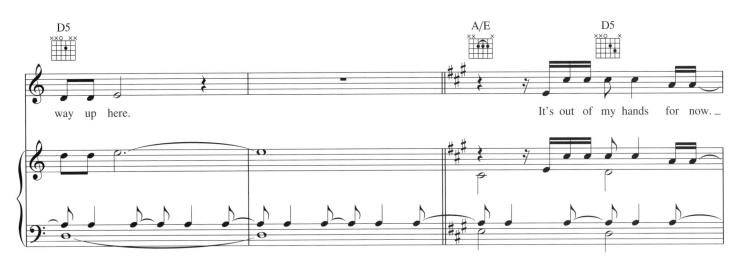

way up here. It's out of my hands for now. ___

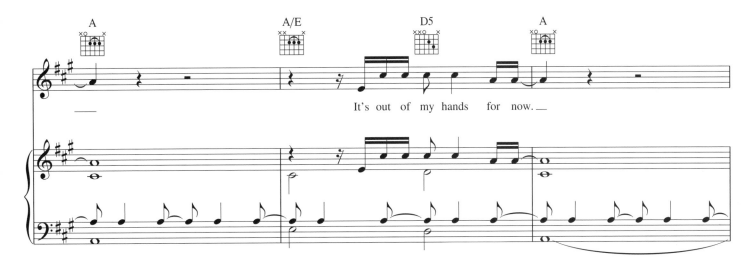

It's out of my hands for now. ___

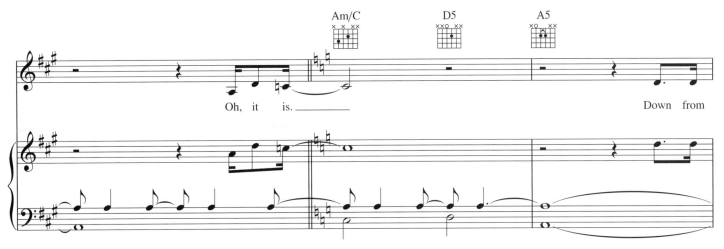

Oh, it is. _____ Down from

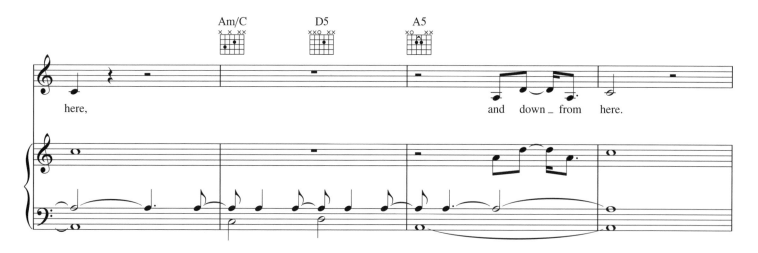

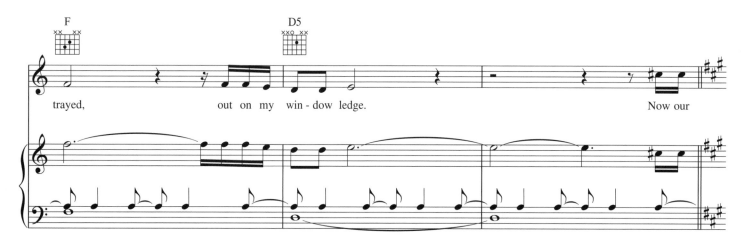

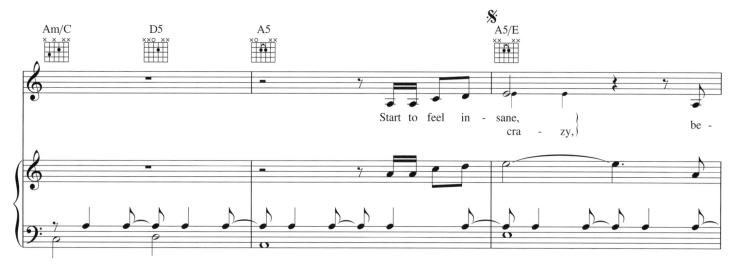

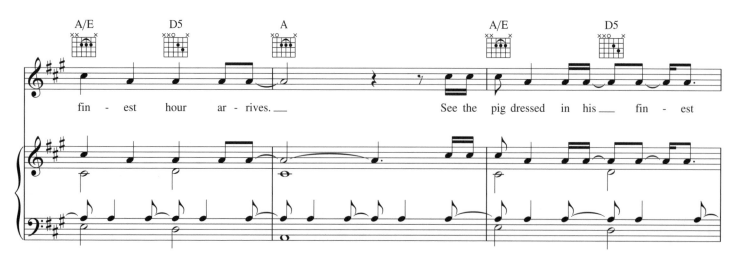

fine. And all \_\_\_ the be - liev - ers stand \_\_\_ be - hind \_\_\_ him and

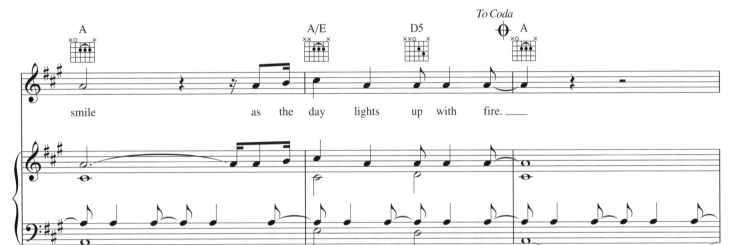

smile as the day lights up with fire. \_\_\_

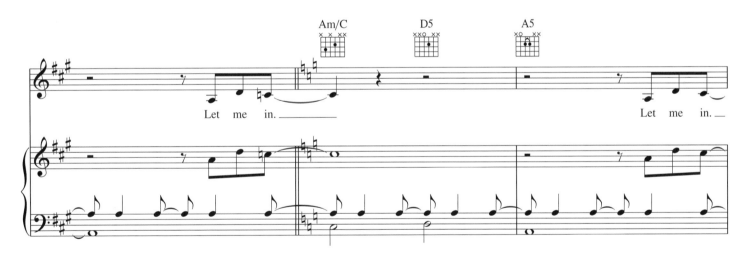

Let me in. _____ Let me in. \_\_\_

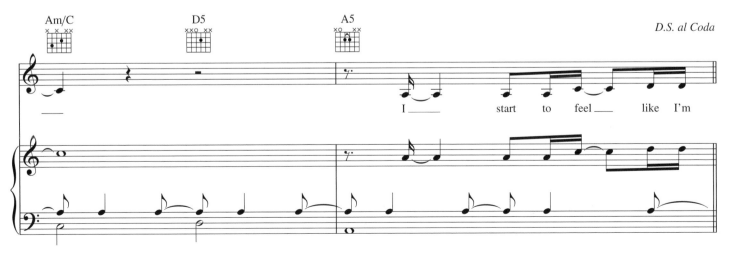

\_\_\_ I \_\_\_ start to feel \_\_\_ like I'm

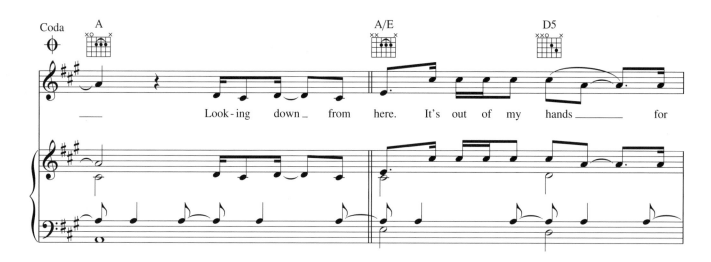

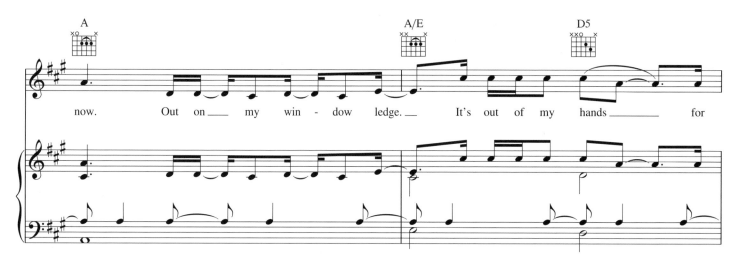

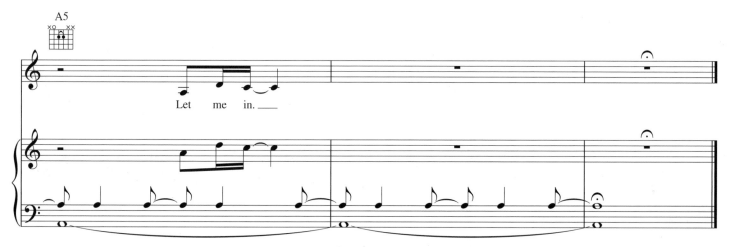

# Rapunzel

Words and Music by
David J. Matthews, Stefan Lessard
and Carter Beauford

**Moderately**

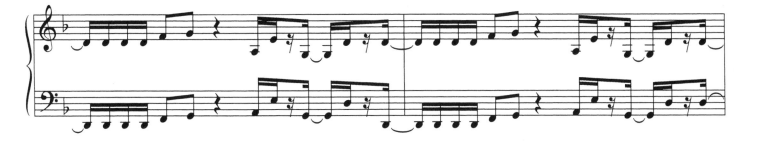

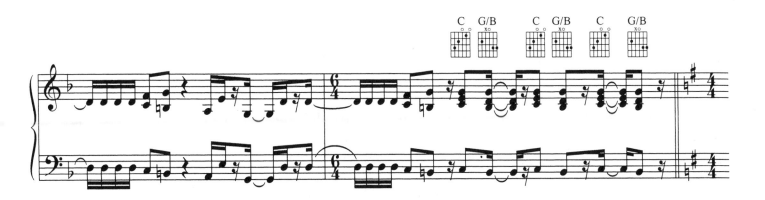

Play 2nd time only

— for— you.

I think— the— world of———— you,————
I think— the— world of———— you,———— with

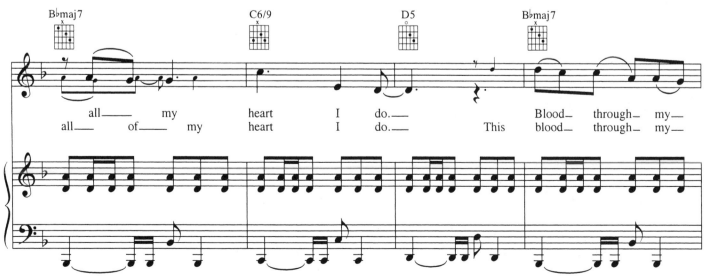

all—— my heart I do.— Blood— through— my—
all— of— my heart I do.— This blood— through— my—

143

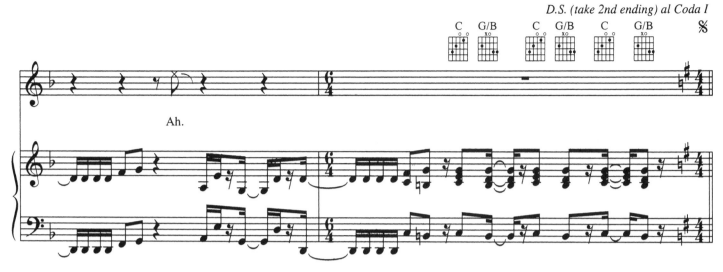

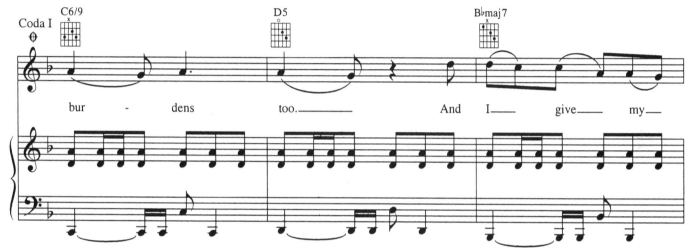

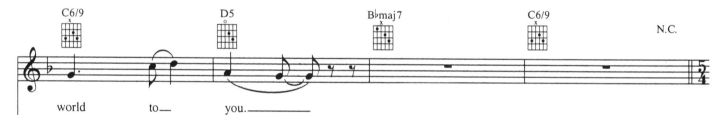

Coda II

Yeah,  yeah,  yeah,  yeah.

*Play 3 times*

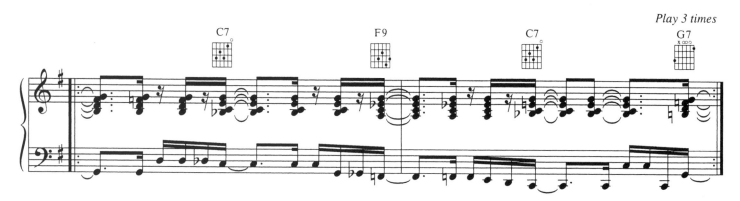

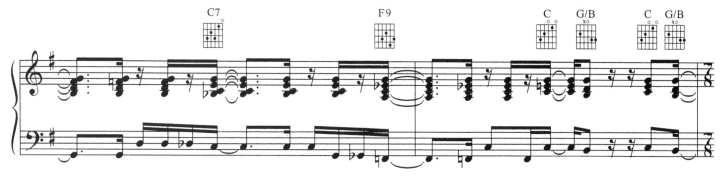

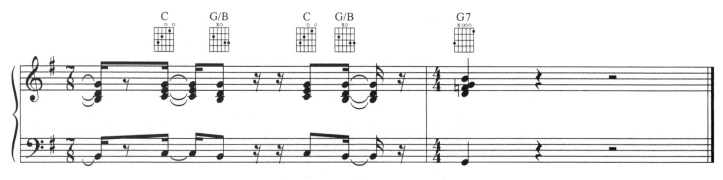

# Satellite

Words and Music by
David J. Matthews

lite strong from the moon, and the world your bal-
lite dish in my yard, and tell me more, tell me

loon. Peep-ing Tom for the moth-er sta-tion.
more. Who's the king of your sat-el-lite cas-tle?

Ab   Db6/9   Bbm7   Eb7sus4

Win-ter's cold, spring e-ras es.

Ab   Db6/9   Bbm7   Eb7sus4

And the calm, a-way by the storm is chas-

en. Ev - 'ry - thing good needs re - plac - ing.____

Look up, look down,____ all a - round. Hey,____ sat - el - lite.

Sat - el -

*To Coda*

# Say Goodbye

Words and Music by
David J. Matthews

bright. (1.) Oh,___ and in your eyes I see___ what's on___ my___

2. *See additional lyrics*

___ mind.___ And you got___ me wild,___ turned a - round in -

side. And oh,___ and then___ de - si - re, see,___ is creep - ing up heav -

(2.)3. *See additional lyrics*

y, ah, in - side here,_____ and the way I

**A**

feel— the same way as I— do— now.— Let's make— this an— eve-

**E**          **D**

ning.          Lov-ers— for a— night,— lov-ers— for—

**A**          Chorus
              **Bm**

— to-night,— for us.— Stay— here— with—
              (2.) Run a-way— here— with—

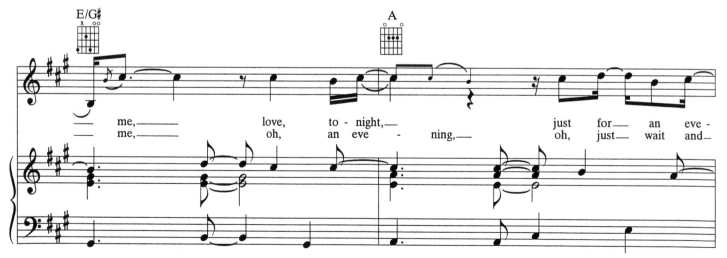

**E/G#**          **A**

— me,— love, to-night,— just for an eve-
— me,— oh, an eve - ning,— oh, just wait and—

154

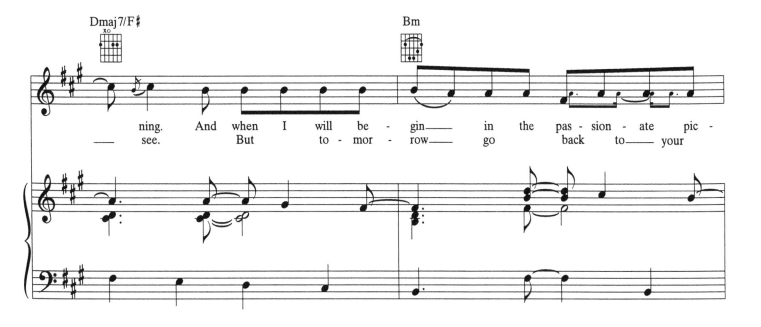

ning. And when I will be - gin_____ in the pas - sion - ate pic -
_____ see. But to - mor - row_____ go back to_____ your

tures, you and me twist_____ up, a - se - cret crea -
man. I'm back to my world_____ and_____ we're back to be -

tures. And we'll stay_____ here,_____ to -

urs. Till— the sun— comes, it's all— ours.— On our way—

—  here. Come— to - mor - row,— go back to be - ing

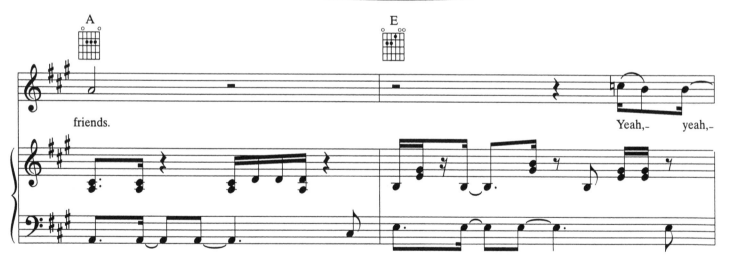

friends.                                                                    Yeah,– yeah,–

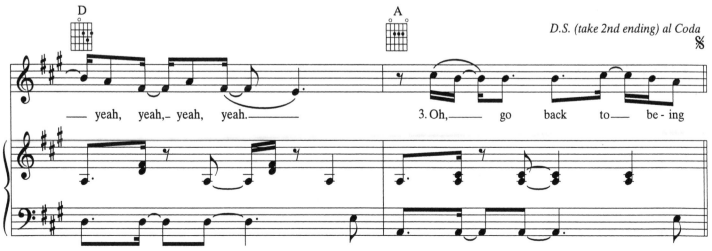

— yeah, yeah,– yeah, yeah.—               3. Oh,— go back to— be - ing

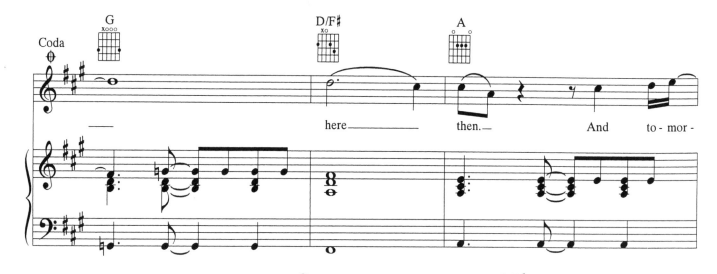

here _____ then. ___ And to-mor-

row ___ back ___ to be-ing _____ friends. ___ Yeah, but now, ___

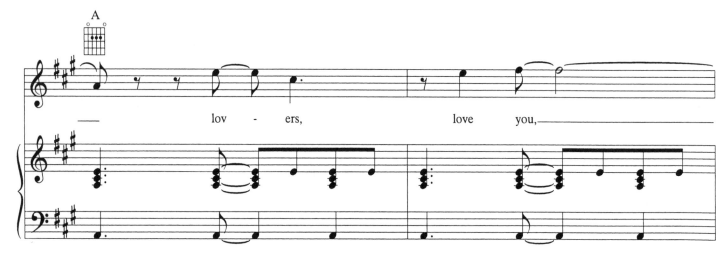

___ lov - ers, love you, _____

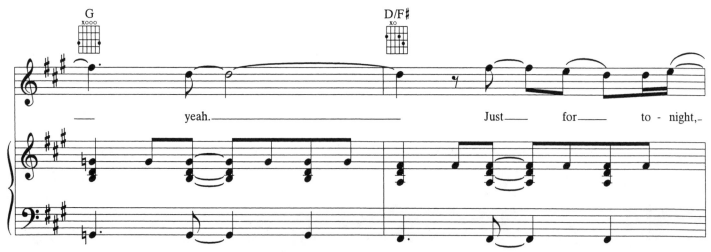

___ yeah. _____ Just ___ for ___ to - night, ___

one night, love you,

yeah, oh.

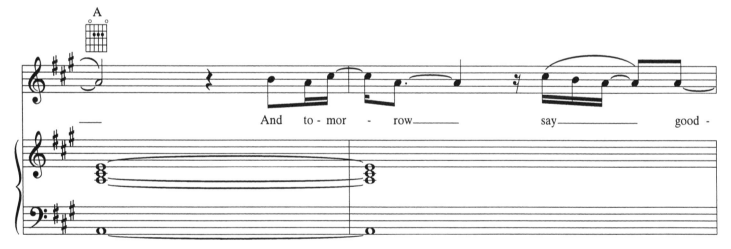

And to - mor - row say good -

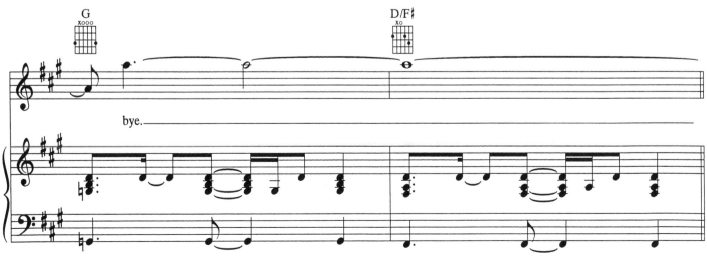

bye.

*Additional Lyrics*

2. Oh, go back to being friends,
   But tonight let's be lovers.
   We kiss and sweat.
   We'll turn this better thing
   To the best
   Of all we can offer.
   Oh, this rogue kiss,
   Tangled tongues and lips.
   See me this way.
   I'm turnin' and turnin' for you.
   Girl, just tonight. *(To Chorus)*

3. Oh, go back to being friends.
   Tonight let's be lovers.
   Oh, please, tonight let's be lovers.
   Say ya will, tonight let's be lovers.
   Oh yeah, tonight let's be lovers.

   *3rd Chorus:*
   And hear me call
   Soft-spoken, whispering love.
   A thing or two I have to say here.
   Tonight, let's go all the way, then,
   Love, I'll see you just for an evening.
   Let's strip down, trip out at this.
   One evening all starts with a kiss.
   And away... *(To Coda)*

# So Much to Say

Words and Music by
David J. Matthews, Boyd Tinsley
and Peter Griesar

see the light. O-pen— up my head— and— let— me

out,— a-lit-tle ba - by.— 'Cause here we have been stand-ing for a

long, long,— time.—

Tread-ing trod-den trails for a long, long,— time.—

164

# So Right

Words and Music by
David J. Matthews and Glen Ballard

168

mor - row _____ we may die, ____ oh, ____ but to -
on and run _____ the red lights. ____ You know, the game

night we're _____ danc - ing in the fate light. Don't you _____
now is _____ keep it tight. Oh, how

I rob _____ your - self of what you're feel - ing.
love _____ your pret - ty rock - and - roll kiss - es.

Don't rob _____ your - self of all that you could Roll
Come ____ on and stay with me.

all 'cause of you. _____ (It's all 'cause of you.)

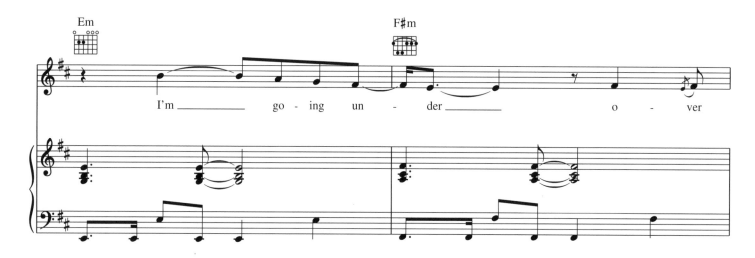

I'm _____ go - ing un - der _____ o - ver

you, o - ver _____ you. _____

*Play 4 times*

This \_\_ time \_\_ is so a - live, \_\_\_ ev - 'ry - bod - y's

trance \_\_\_\_ danc - ing to - night. Oh, \_\_\_ so

beau - ti - ful \_\_\_\_\_ and so strange. Oh, it was emp-

G/B

ty un - til you came. \_\_ Our \_\_ love \_\_ is

Dmaj7

174

rain down on ____ you. Our love is so right. ____

Don't ___ be - lieve, ___ don't be - lieve ___ the rain, ___ oh. ____

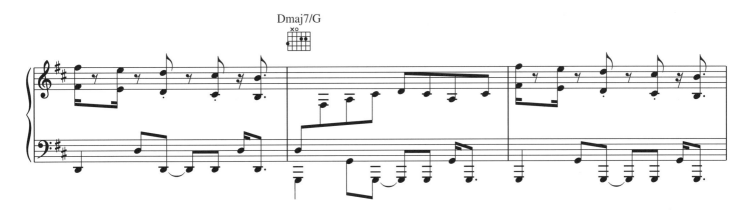

*Repeat and fade*

# The Space Between

Words and Music by
David J. Matthews and Glen Ballard

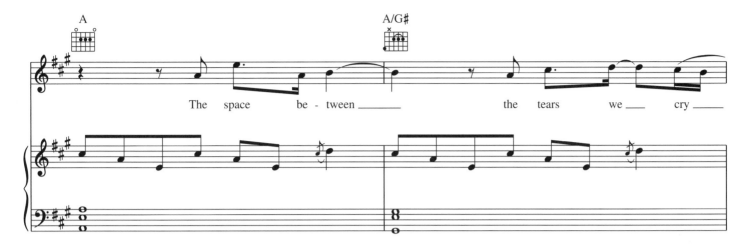

The space be-tween _____ the tears we _ cry _____

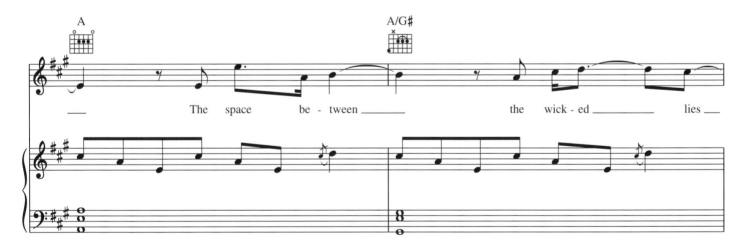

_ is the laugh-ter keeps _ us com-ing back _ for more. _

_ The space be-tween _____ the wick-ed _____ lies _

_ we tell _____ and hope _____ to keep us safe from the pain. ___

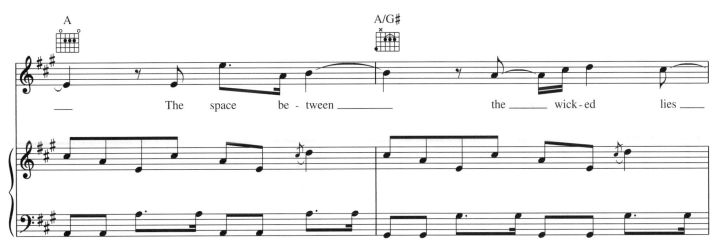

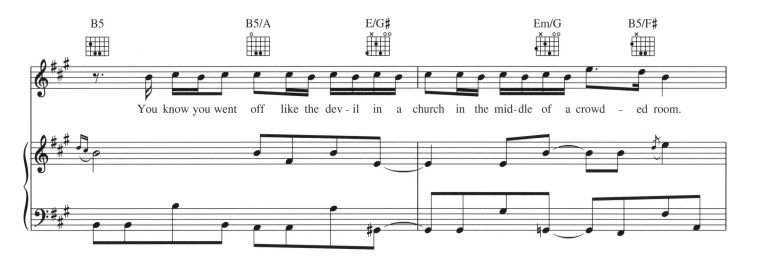

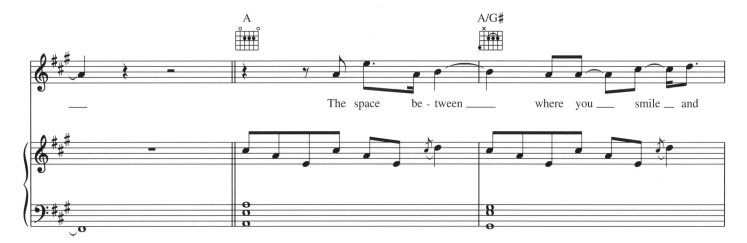

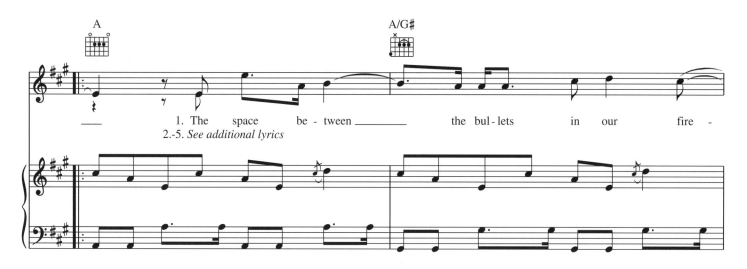

A          A/G♯

1. The space be-tween _____ the bul-lets in our fire-

*2.-5. See additional lyrics*

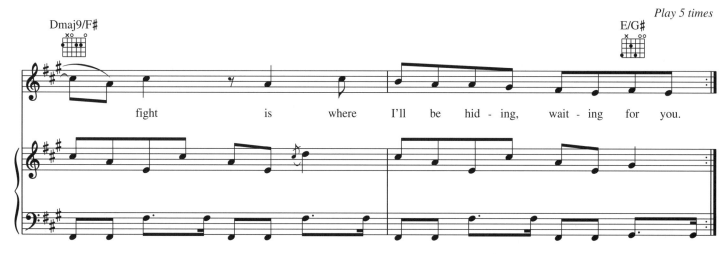

*Play 5 times*

Dmaj9/F♯          E/G♯

fight is where I'll be hid - ing, wait - ing for you.

A          A/G♯          Dmaj9/F♯

The space be-tween what's wrong and right is where you'll find

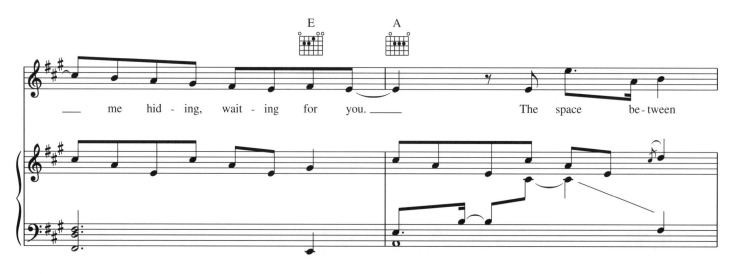

E          A

me hid - ing, wait - ing for you. The space be - tween

your ___ heart and ___ mine _____ is the space _

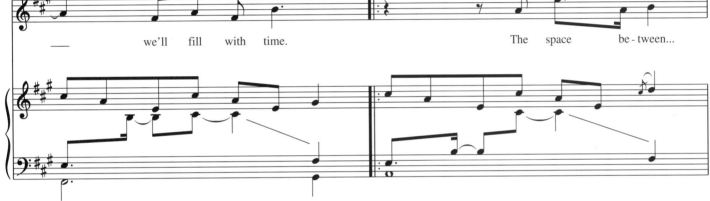

___ we'll fill with time. The space be - tween...

*Repeat and fade*

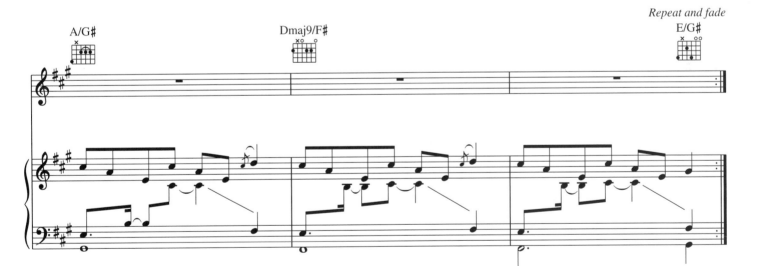

*Additional Lyrics*

2. The rain that falls splashed in your heart,
   Ran like sadness down the window into your room.

3. The space between our wicked lies is where
   We hope to keep safe from pain.

4. Take my hand 'cause
   We're walking out of here.

5. Oh, right out of here.
   Love is all we need, dear.

# Stay

## (Wasting Time)

Words and Music by
David J. Matthews, Stefan Lessard
and Leroi Moore

**Moderately**

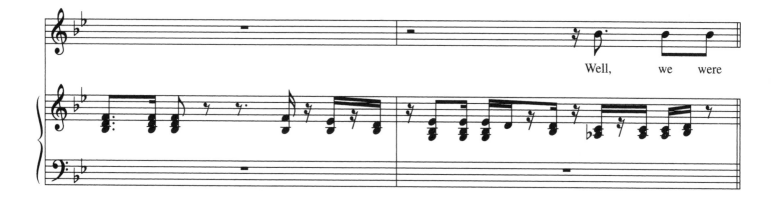

Well,     we    were

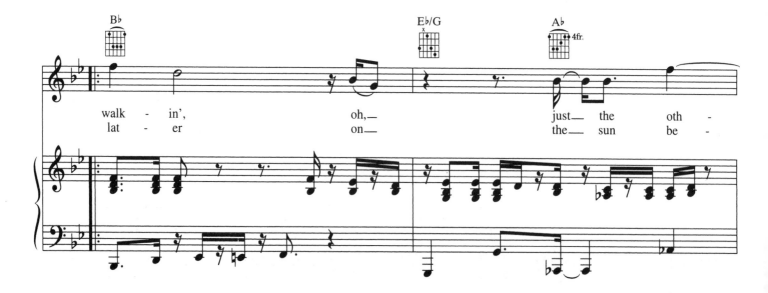

walk -  in',                oh,            just    the     oth -

lat -  er                  on            the    sun     be -

your face.        Reached up           and      I
in'       in the tongue      taste.          And for a

caught  it  at  your     chin,        licked  my   fin - ger-
mo - ment, this your good    time        would   nev - er

tips.            We  were        we were      just
end.       You and me,       you  and  me      just

wast -      in'      time.         Let  the ho-
wast -      in'      time.         I was kiss -

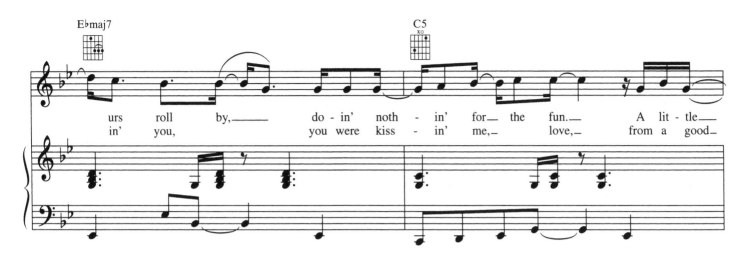

urs roll by,\_\_\_ do - in' noth - in' for the fun.\_ A lit - tle\_
in' you, you were kiss - in' me,\_ love,\_ from a good\_

\_\_ taste of the good\_\_\_ life, wheth - er right\_
\_\_ day in - to\_\_ the moon - light. Now a night\_

1.

\_\_ or wrong,\_\_\_ makes us wan - na stay, stay,\_ stay,\_
\_\_ so fine\_\_\_ makes us wan - na

\_\_ stay, stay\_ for a while.\_

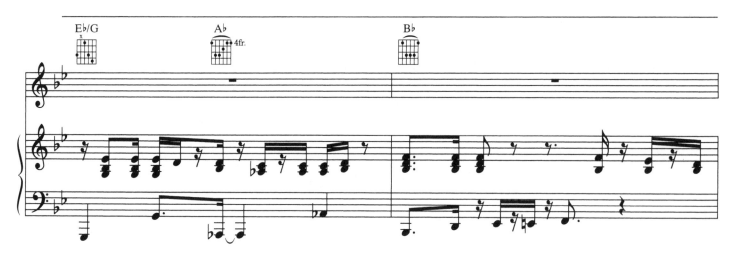

Well, then stay, stay, stay,

stay, stay for a while.

(Makes you wan - na, makes you wan - na...

Makes— me wan - na, makes me wan - na...

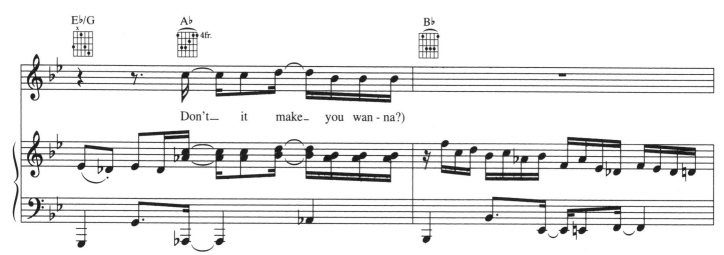

Don't— it make— you wan - na?)

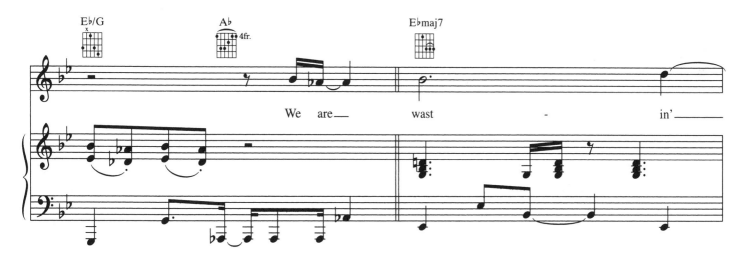

We are— wast - in'—

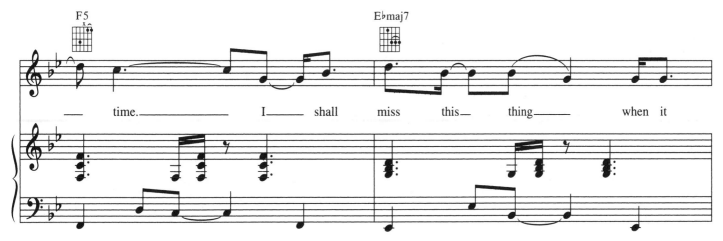

— time.— I— shall miss this— thing— when it

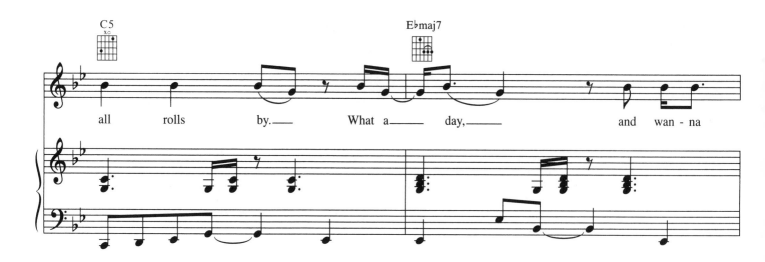

all rolls by.___ What a___ day,___ and wan-na

stay, stay,___ stay,___ stay, stay___ for___ a while.___

*Play 3 times*

*(Sing 1st time only)*

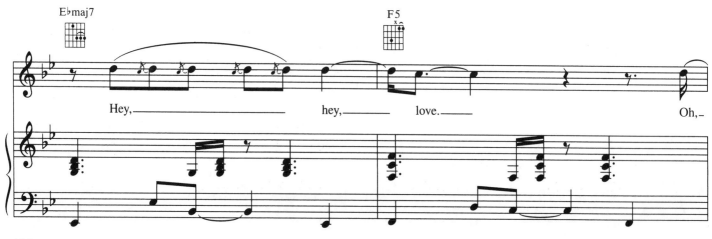

Hey,_____ hey,___ love.___ Oh,–

190

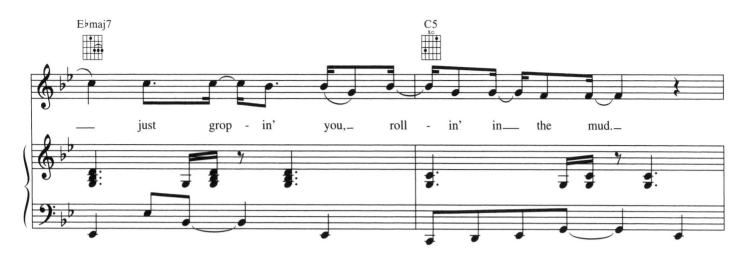

just grop - in' you,— roll - in' in— the mud.—

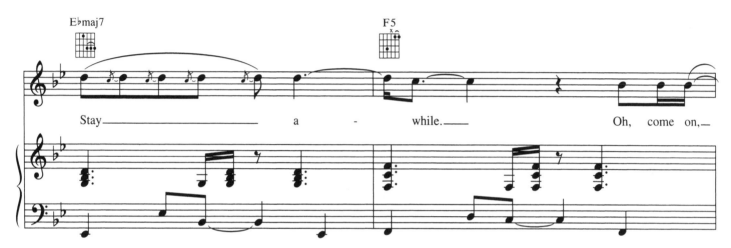

Stay—————————————— a - while.— Oh, come on,—

I wan - na stay, stay,— stay,—

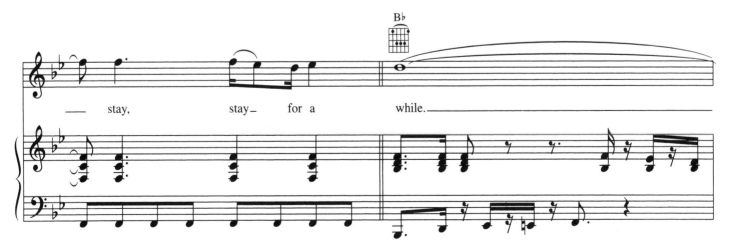

— stay, stay— for a while.—————————

(Makes me wan-na, makes me wan-na stay.

*Play 4 times*

Makes me wan-na, makes me wan-na stay. Don't it

*Play 4 times*

make you wan-na stay!)

# Steady As We Go

Words and Music by
Dave Matthews Band and Mark Batson

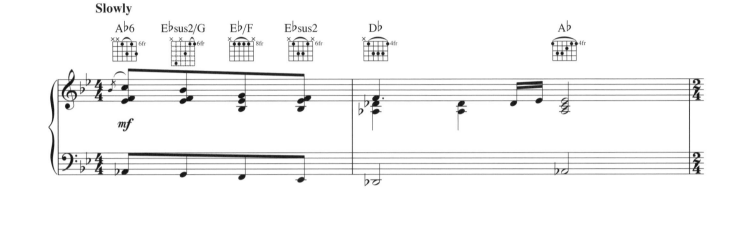

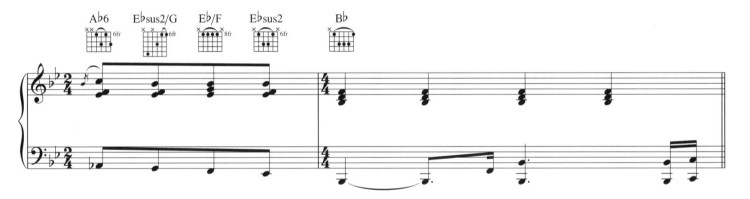

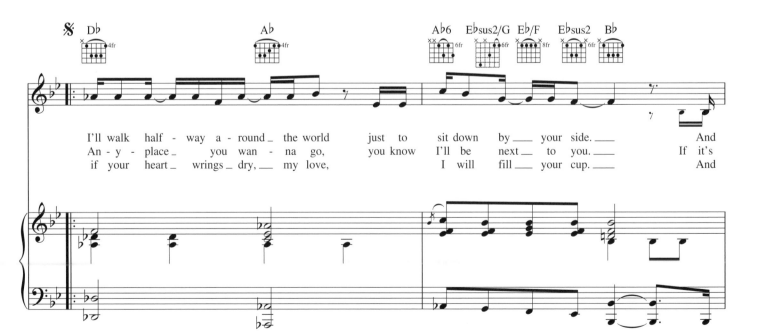

I'll walk half - way a - round _ the world just to sit down by _ your side. _ And
An - y - place _ you wan - na go, you know I'll be next _ to you. _ If it's
if your heart _ wrings _ dry, _ my love, _ I will fill _ your cup. _ And

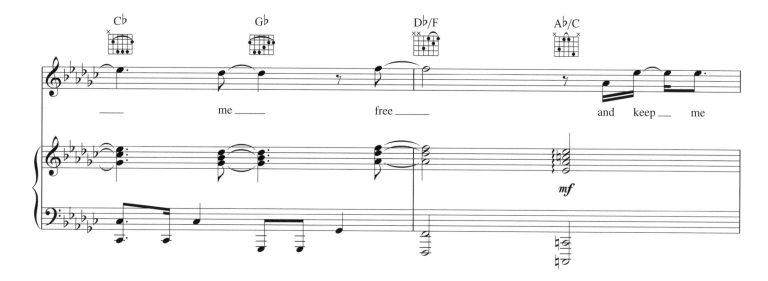

me ____ free ____ and keep ____ me

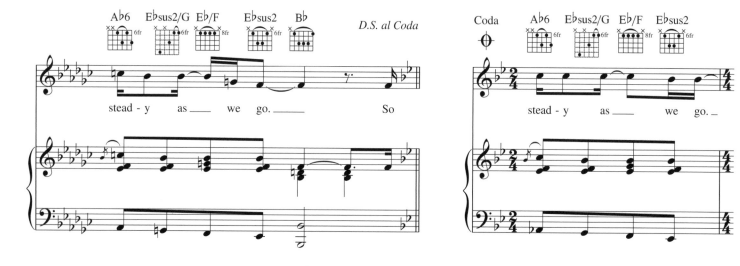

*D.S. al Coda*

stead - y as ____ we go. ____ So

Coda

stead - y as ____ we go. ____

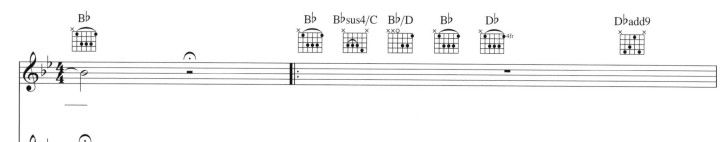

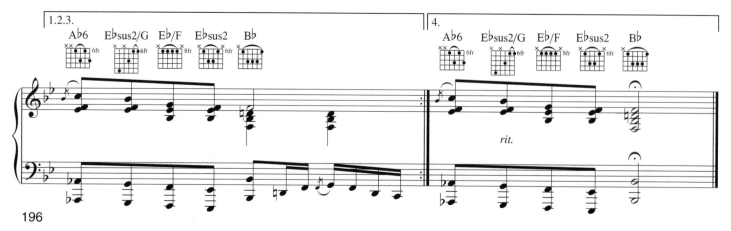

# Too Much

Words by David J. Matthews
Music by David J. Matthews, Carter Beauford,
Stefan Lessard, Leroi Moore
and Boyd Tinsley

Hmm, push it through— the doors———— 'cause— in between— the lines—

— I'm gon-na pack— more——— lines——————— so I can get down in.

F#5

2. Oh, traf-fic jam, got more cars than a beach got sand.
3.4. *See additional lyrics*

Suck it up, suck it up, suck it up. Fill it up un-til no more. I'm no— cra - zy creep.—

198

you nev-er know,_____ may - be— you're_ dream - ing.

Coda I

F#5

Chorus

I eat  too much.  I drink  too much.  I want  too much.

Too much!

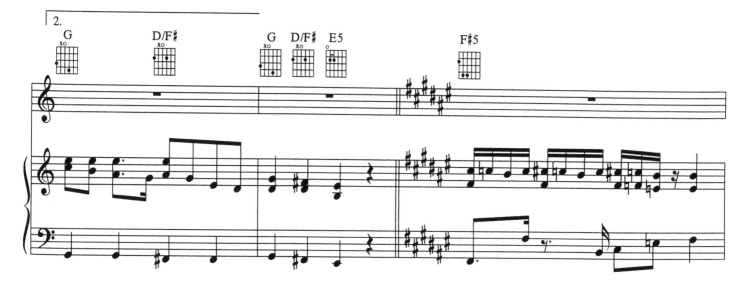

*D.S. al Coda II* 𝄋

Coda II

Too— much!—

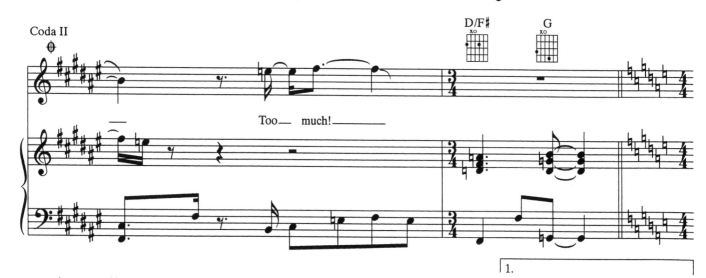

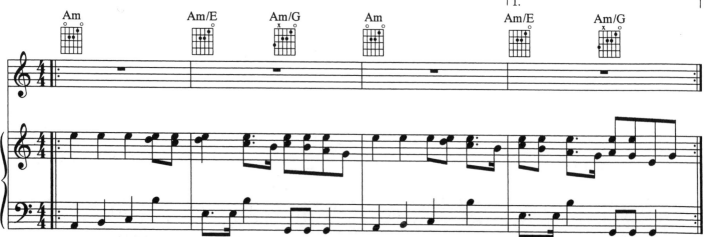

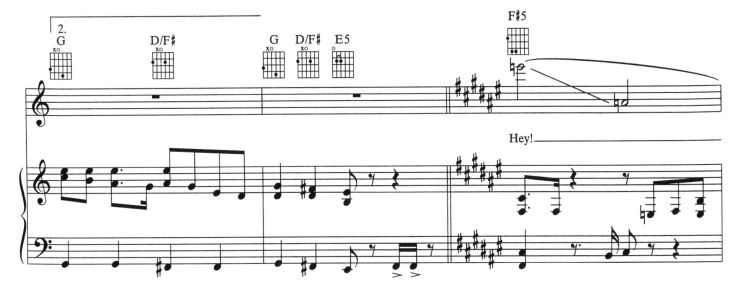

Hey!

Suck it up,    suck it up.

Suck it up,    suck it up,    suck it up, yeah.

Suck it up,—— suck it up, suck it up.

Suck it up, suck it up, suck it up, suck it up, ba - by.

'Cause I eat— too much.— 'Cause I drink— too much.—

'Cause I want— too much.————

Too much!

F#5

*Repeat and fade*

*Additional Lyrics*

2. Who do you think you're watching?
   Who do you think you need?
   Play for me, play more,
   Ten times in the same day.
   I need more.
   I'm going over my borders.
   Gonna take more,
   More from you, letter by letter. *(To Chorus)*

3. I told God, "I'm coming to your country.
   I'm going to eat up your cities,
   Your homes, you know."
   I've got a stomach full.
   It's not a chip on my shoulder.
   I've got this growl in my tummy
   And I'm gonna stop it today. *(To Chorus)*

# Tripping Billies

Words and Music by
David J. Matthews

We were a- bove, you were stand- ing un- der- neath us. We
We're wear- ing noth- ing, noth- ing but our shad- ows. Shad- ows
We are all sit- ting, legs crossed, 'round a fire.

209

210

# Two Step

Words and Music by
David J. Matthews

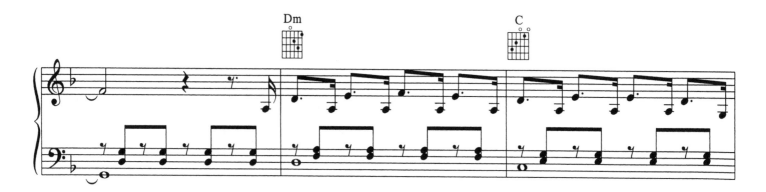

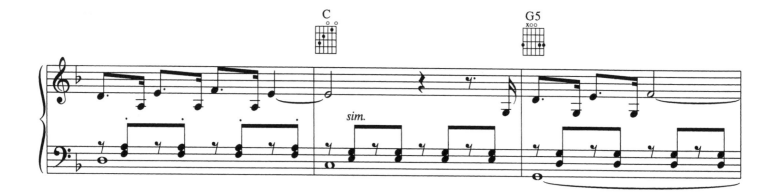

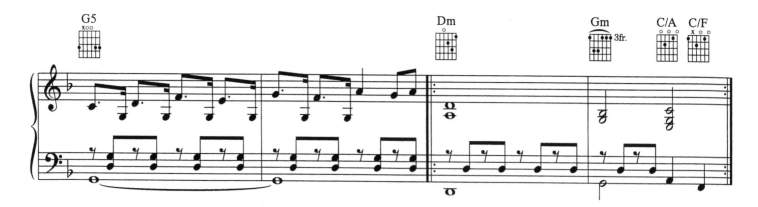

Say,                    my————— love,        I came— to you— with

best              in - ten - tion.—————

You———————         laid————— down        and gave— to me— just

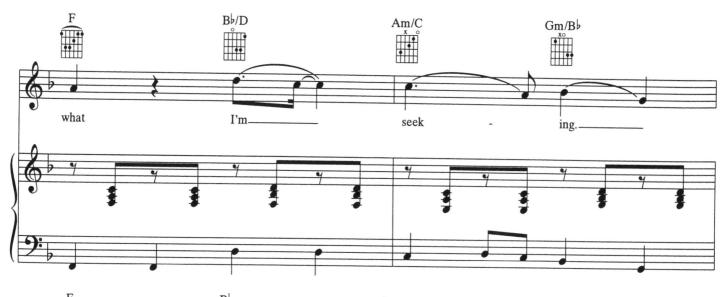

what      I'm_____      seek  -  ing._____

Say,      love,     you___ drive    me      to     dis - trac -

tion.

Oh,_____ hey, my____ love, do you___ be - lieve___ that
Hey,_____ hey, my____ love, you came__ to me___ like
Oh,_____ how, my____ love, I came__ to you___ with

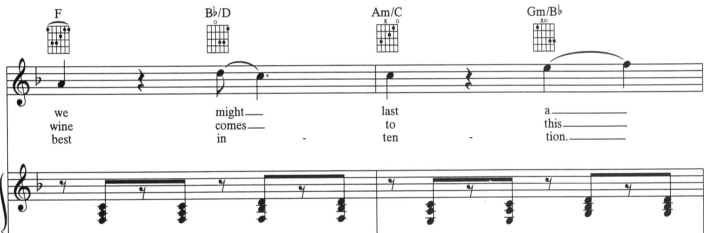

we might____ last to a_____
wine comes____ in - ten - this_____
best in - ten - tion._____

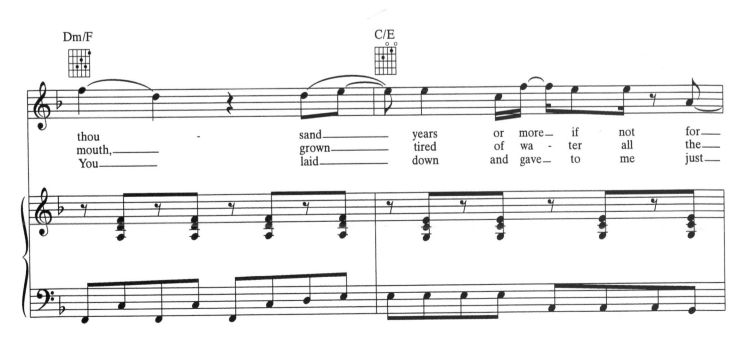

thou - sand_____ years or more___ if not for___
mouth,_____ grown_____ tired of wa - ter all the___
You_____ laid_____ down and gave___ to me just___

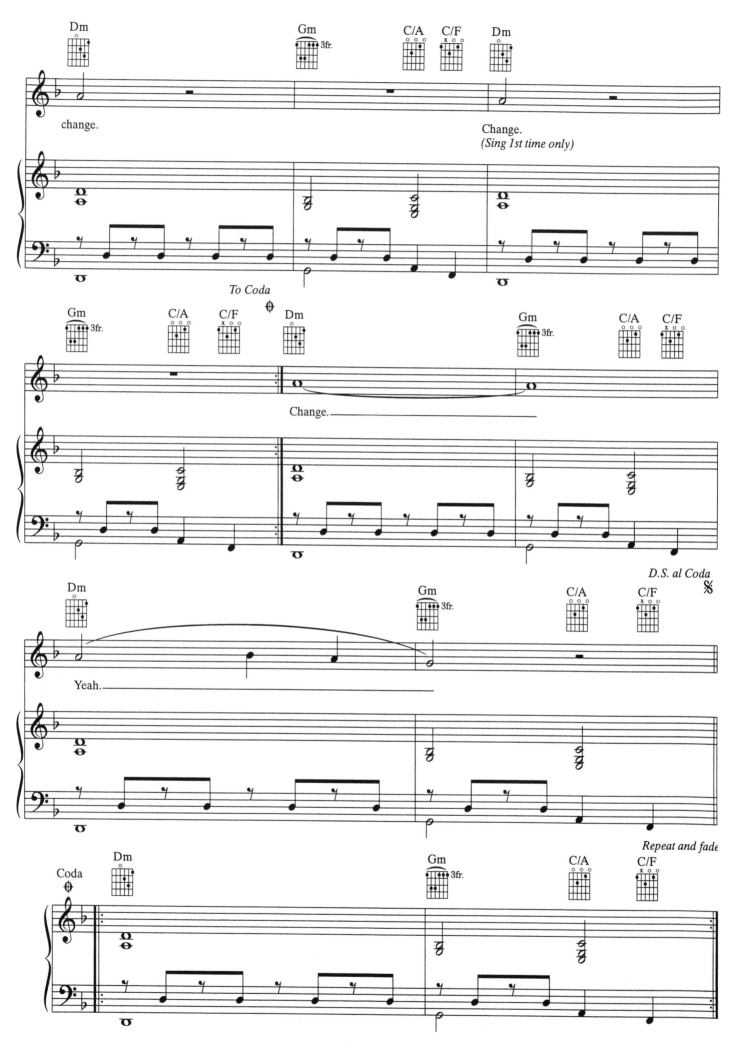

change.                                        Change.
                                               (Sing 1st time only)

Change.

Yeah.

# Warehouse

Words and Music by
David J. Matthews

Has me tied up in knots,————————— can't——— test for a mo - ment.

Soon I'm go - in',—————————————————

————————————————— ooh, I'm slip - pin' slow a - way.

Hop - in' to find some - thing bet - ter——— than I've

got in - side of here._____ And the ware - house slips

Bm

a - way._____
*(Sing 1st time only)*

Bm

*Play 3 times*

Hey! A

reck - less___ mind,_____ don't throw___ be -
We have___ found_____ be com -
I'm think - ing_____ I had___

___ a - way___ your play - ful be - gin - nings.
ing___ one___ in a mil - lion slip in -
___ a___ clue,___ now it's gone___ for - ev - er. Sit - ting

You and___ I_____ will fum - ble a - round in the
to the___ crowd._____ This ques - tion I found in the
o - ver___ these bones,___ you can read in what - ev - er you're

touch - es. And be sure to leave___ all___ the lights on so we___ can see the
gap in the side - walk. Keep___ all___ your sights on. Hey, the
need - in' to. Keep___ all___ your sights on. Yeah___ man, the

222

black cat chang - ing— col - ors.———— And we— can
black cat chang - ing— col - ors.———— And we— can
black cat chang - ing— col - ors———— when it's not the

walk un - der——— lad - ders,——— and
walk un - der——— lad - ders,——— and
col - ors— that——— mat - ter,——— but that they

1.

swim as— the— tide——————— turns— you a - round and a - round,— a -
swim as— the— tide———
all fade— a — way,———

Bm

2.

3

round. Hey! —— choose to turn you.
—— yeah, yeah, yeah. And

And here I— sit. } Life goes— on. End of tun-nel, T V— set, spot-
I..._____ |

— in the mid-dle. Stat-ic fade, sta-tis-ti-cal bit. And soon I'll— fade a-

way,— I'll fade a-way.___ Oh,— but this I— ad-mit. { Tastes—
                                                      { Seems—

— so— good, hard to be-lieve an end to it. Smell,—
— so— good, hard to be-lieve an end to it. The

My love, I'd love to stay here.

My love, I'd   In a cor-ner, was won-d'ring

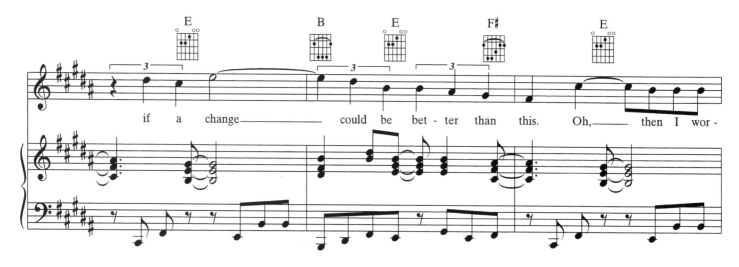

if a change _____ could be bet-ter than this. Oh, _____ then I wor-

ry   may-be things ___ won't be   bet-ter   than they have ___

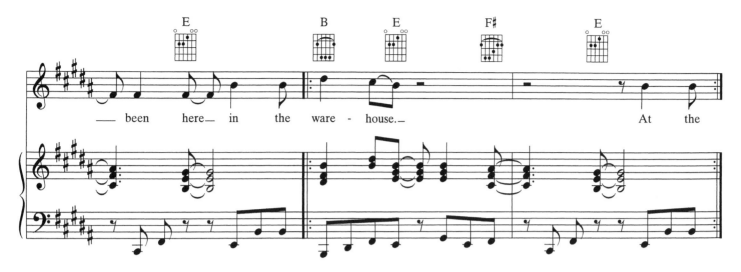

been here— in the ware - house.— At the

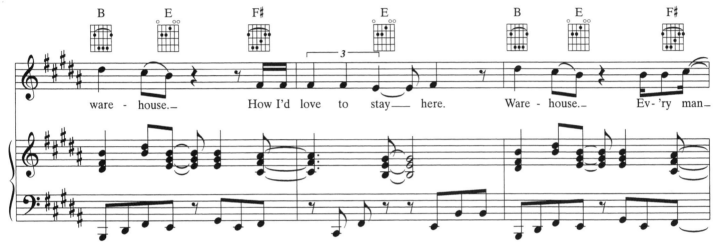

ware - house.— How I'd love to stay— here. Ware - house.— Ev-'ry man—

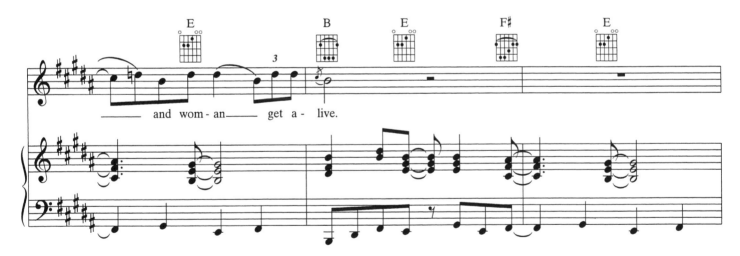

——— and wom-an— get a - live.

Ooh,— that's our— blood——— down there.—

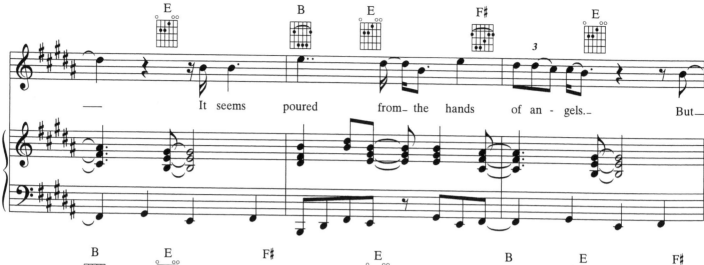

It seems poured from the hands of an - gels. But—

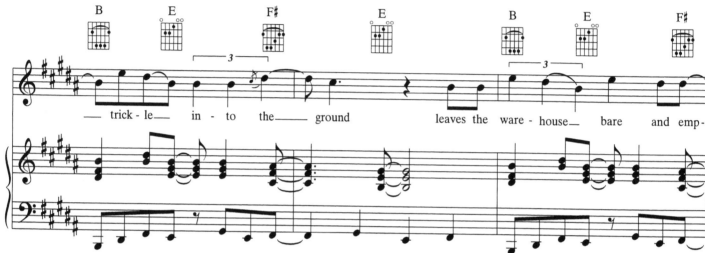

trick - le— in - to the— ground leaves the ware - house— bare and emp-

ty. And my heart's— num - bered beat— still ech-

o in this— emp - ty room. And fear— wells in—

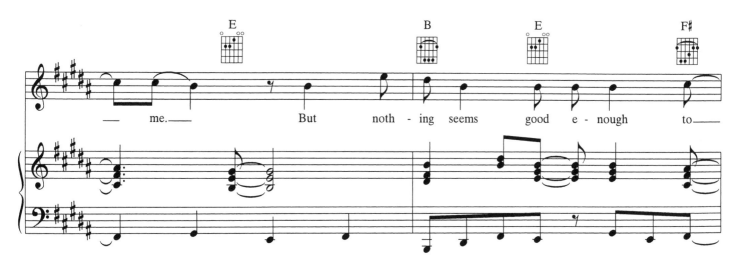

me.___ But noth-ing seems good e-nough to___

___de - fend.___ So I'm go-ing a - way,___ I'm go-ing a - way,___

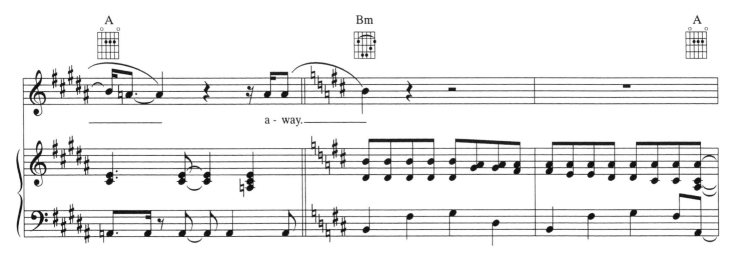

a - way.___

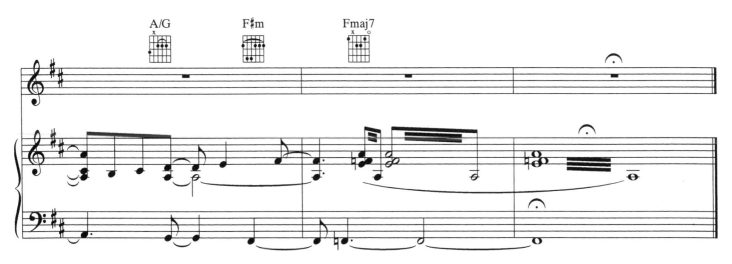

# What Would You Say

Words and Music by
David J. Matthews

Up and down the pup-pies' hair, fleas and ticks jump ev-a-
I was there when the bear ate his head, it thought it was a

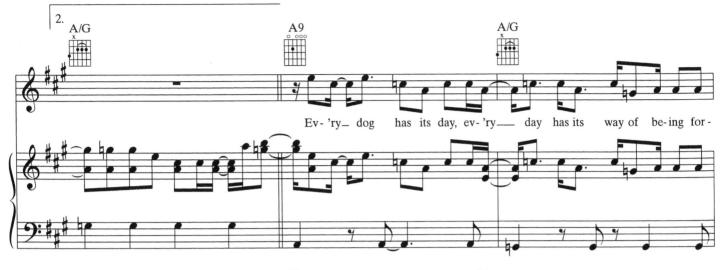

Ev-'ry— dog has its day, ev-'ry— day has its way of be-ing for-

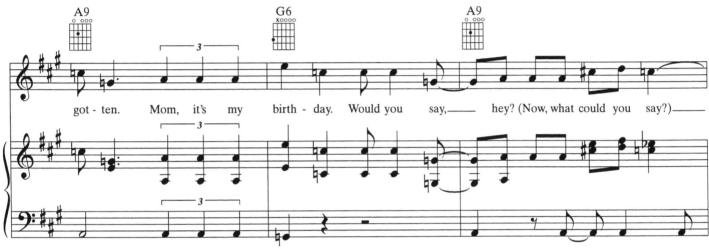

got - ten. Mom, it's my birth - day. Would you say,— hey? (Now, what could you say?)—

—— What— would you say?—

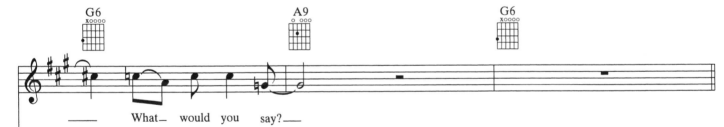

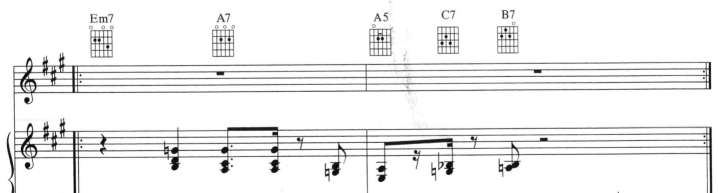

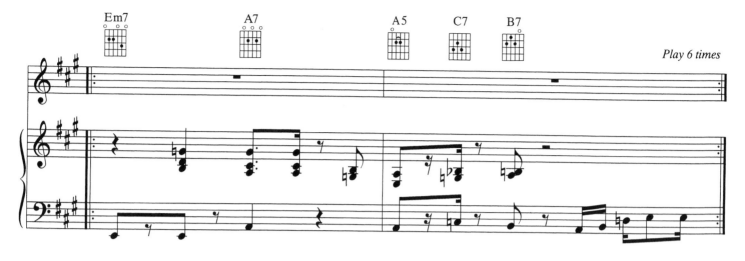

*Play 6 times*

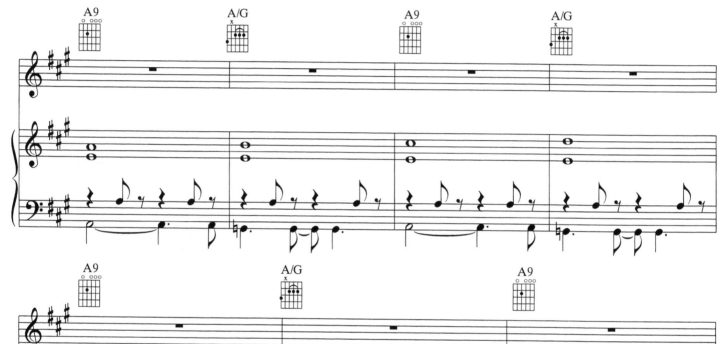

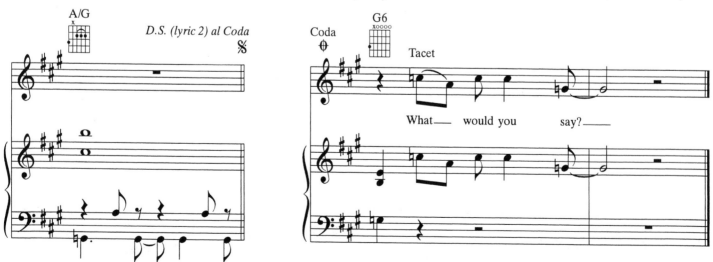

*D.S. (lyric 2) al Coda* 𝄋

Coda

Tacet

What— would you say?—

234

# Where Are You Going

Lyrics by David J. Matthews

Music by Dave Matthews Band

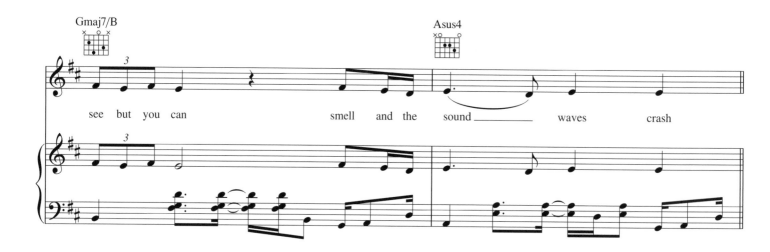

see but you can smell and the sound _____ waves crash

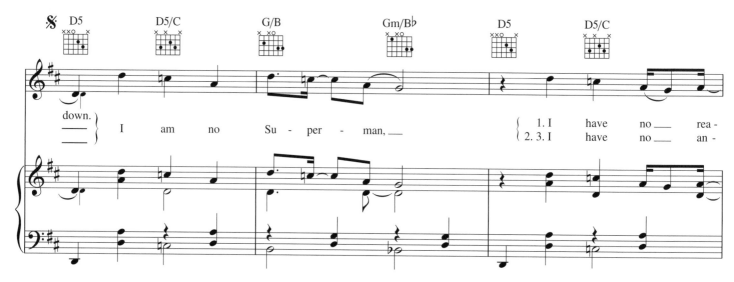

down. I am no Su - per - man, _____
1. I have no _____ rea -
2. 3. I have no _____ an -

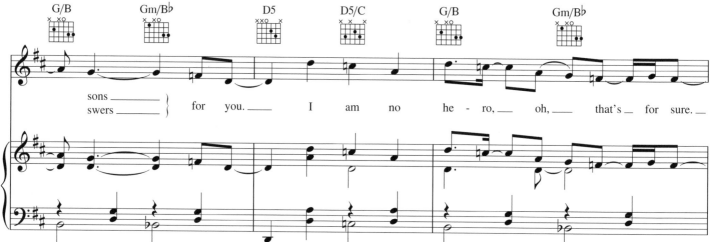

sons _____ for you. _____ I am no he - ro, _____ oh, _____ that's _____ for sure. _____
swers _____

But I do _____ know _____ one thing is where you

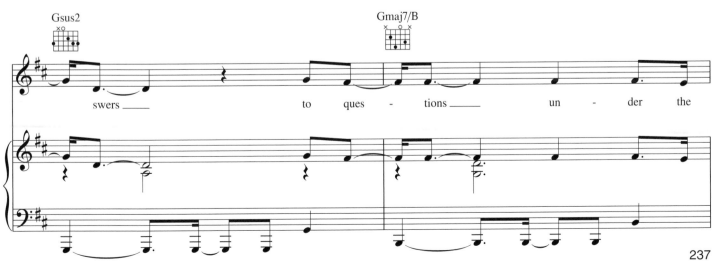

stars? Well, if a - long the way _____ you are grow - ing wea -

*D.S. al Coda I*

ry, you can rest with me un - til a bright - er day and you're o - kay. _____

Coda I

_____ Where are you go - ing?

Where do you go? _____

Where do you go? _____ Tell me, where are you go-

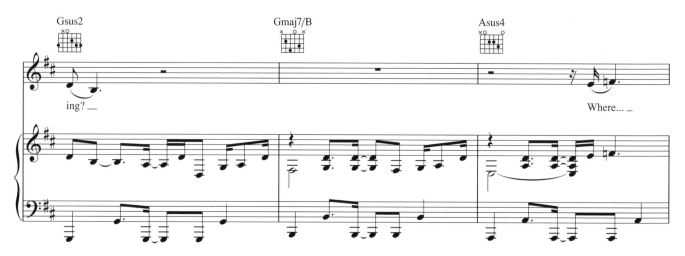

ing? __ Where... _

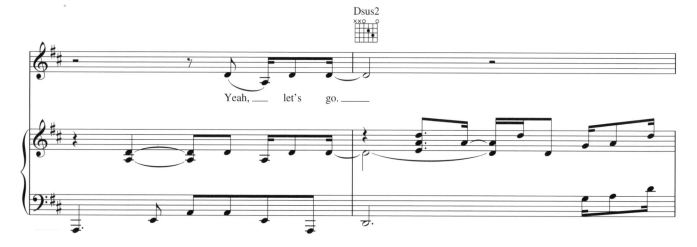

Yeah, __ let's go. _____